DYNAMIC DU♥S

The essential guide for couples in business together

Julie Richman

INDEPENDENT

First published 2018 by Independent Ink
PO Box 1638, Carindale
Queensland 4152 Australia
independentink.com.au

Copyright © Julie Richman 2018

All rights reserved. Except as permitted under the *Australian Copyright Act 1968*, no part of this publication may be reproduced, stored in a retrieval system, or transmitted in any form or by any means, electronic, mechanical, photocopying, recording or otherwise, without prior written permission from the publisher. All enquiries should be made to the author.

Cover design by Julia Kuris
Edited by Michele Perry
Internal design by Independent Ink
Typeset in 9.75/17 pt Helvetica Neue by Post Pre-press Group, Brisbane

A catalogue record for this book is available from the National Library of Australia

ISBN 978-0-648224-0-2

Disclaimer:
Any information in the book is purely the opinion of the author based on personal experience and should not be taken as business or legal advice. All material is provided for educational purposes only. We recommend to always seek the advice of a qualified professional before making any decision regarding personal and business needs.

CONTENTS

ACKNOWLEDGMENTS — vii
FOREWORD — 1
PREFACE — 3

INTRODUCTION — 7
    Clues that things are going wrong — 8
    The beginning — 9
    Universal laws — 10

SECTION ONE – ESSENTIAL BASELINE — 15
    The Five Cs — 16
    The Five Core Living Principles — 17

SECTION TWO – CLARITY — 31
    Who are you as a couple? — 35
    What is your purpose together? — 36
    Is there imbalance in your love? — 38
    How do you differ from one another? — 40

What is your role in the relationship?	52
What is your role in the business?	54
SECTION THREE – COMMITMENT	**61**
Attitude and ability	63
Understanding compatibility and acceptance	64
Understanding individuality and togetherness	65
Applying balance and acceptance	67
Combining your visions and values	68
Love and intimacy	69
Why couples argue	95
SECTION FOUR – COMMUNICATION	**109**
What is effective communication?	111
Signs of communication disaster	114
Emotional arguments	114
Venting	115
Listening without judgement	116
Classic motion	116
We all make mistakes	118
One person speaking at a time	120
Appreciation and validation	123
Agree to disagree– talking about the tough stuff	124
The good, bad and ugly	129
The tough life	130
Ten minutes of 100% focus	132
The secret to 'love'	135

SECTION FIVE – COOPERATION	139
Self-directed leadership	140
Systemising the business	141
Roles and responsibilities	150
Work-free zones	152
Working together without conflict	154
Effective teamwork	157
Being responsible – accepting that we all make mistakes / Being accountable – taking action	161
Listen to advice from others	164
SECTION SIX – COLLABORATION	169
Creating common visions	170
Assessing milestones and targets – rewarding yourselves	175
Setting goals and stepping back	179
Building a successful business	181
Increasing profits	182
Peak performance teams	184
Growing together	186
Exit strategy	189
SUMMARY	191
ADDITIONAL INFORMATION	195

ACKNOWLEDGMENTS

I could not have written this book without my knowledge and experiences; as well as receiving input from people around me, who have helped create those experiences – good, bad and indifferent.

Personally, my husband William is by far the most supportive and loving husband anyone could wish for. I want to thank him for being the wonderful man that he is. Thank you to my daughters, Shannen and Michelle, my sister Helen, and all my family, as well as all my dear and long-time friends.

Thank you to Andrew Griffiths for his contributions and for being a wonderful publishing mentor. Thank you to Jacqui Pretty for her great assistance in the structure of this book, Michael Hanrahan for his honest feedback, and all the leadership team and members of the KPI group for supporting my writing process. Thanks also to my BG7 Group who have been through this journey with me. Without their feedback and ideas, writing this book would have been so much harder.

I would also like to thank Ann Wilson and Michele Perry for their support and guidance through the compiling and creation of this book, and a huge thank you to Julia Kuris for her patience through the cover design process. Thanks to Jo Rahn at Zanthii PR and Communications for your support, and Dyon Swanborough for your technical application in breathing life into the 'Dynamic Duos' vision and dream.

Most of all, I would like to thank the readers, and the couples in business who work hard and live together embracing their myriad of experiences every day.

FOREWORD

Julie Richman came into our lives ten years ago. She was introduced to me by a speaker I'd heard at a business seminar, and I quickly realised that this young woman had a mental age far beyond her years, and she helped us in many ways.

Julie was a business coach, as well as a life coach, and she demonstrated time and again that she could grasp an issue and come up with a solution that solved the problem. Julie quickly understood our business and our culture, and we found our regular meetings with her invaluable.

My wife and I had worked together when we first met in London in 1975, and we married in 1978. In 1981, we moved to Australia, and she and I worked on her parents' sheep station in northern New South Wales, for about six months before moving to Sydney.

There we worked separately until around 1983, when we set up a business in which we were both involved. We had two children in

1984 and 1985, and in 1987 we moved to Brisbane. During those early years, my wife gave up work to raise our son and daughter.

In 1995, we again created a business as a boutique property agency in Brisbane, and we worked together in this business until we recently separated. Being together day in and day out for over 23 years was no easy thing, especially with the day-to-day stress of staff and cash flow, which were primarily her domain.

The relationship became one of taking each other for granted and, over time, it became stale. In 2017, when our relationship dissolved, it was a very difficult time for my wife and family, and for me also.

I have had several conversations with Julie since our separation, and I know that she would have been the ideal person to have asked for help at the time.

I would urge anyone who is going through a rocky period to get help as soon as possible.

I wish I had.
D.D.

PREFACE

For most of my life I have moved around from place to place. I went to nine different schools and so never really had a good group of friends that I could bond with for any length of time. Making friends in a new country and new school was very hard, and I was shy.

My deepest wish has always been for people to just accept others for who they are, and not to change anything about them. I also wish for people to have genuine appreciation for others, and to understand that we are all human beings, we all make mistakes and are doing the best we can with what we know.

We can all be a little prickly and a little sweet, just like a pineapple. We each have our good points and our rough edges – some green, some ripe and some rotten – but at the end of the day, we are all the same: human.

My first marriage and business almost killed me. We owned and ran a franchise together for three and a half years. When our marriage and business ended, I was left emotionally, spiritually and financially destitute. Based upon the fairytales we all tell our children, the concept that I would grow up and meet my prince charming and live happily ever after was shattered at the ripe old age of thirty. So I did what I normally would do, from my tragically unstable childhood, I picked myself up and dusted myself off, and I started again.

The second time around with marriage and business combined, I was much wiser. I knew many of the pitfalls that happened within relationships, and so I could apply better strategies into making things work a lot smoother.

Combined with my knowledge about owning and operating a busy suburban coffee shop, and my general experience in business, my new husband and I made a great start in our business venture together.

He has technical skills to fix machines, and I can see the bigger picture about where and how to make the business grow. So we combined these strengths and now run a business that services office equipment for other small businesses. Our support helps their business to flourish. To be a part of other people's success in business is truly rewarding.

Much of my own personal journey is reflected in the steps to a stronger relationship that I share within this book. My divorce, business failures, self-reflections, and learning to love and trust again are all a big part to that journey.

I had to dig deep within to discover and recognise the key areas that build a successful 'husband' and 'wife' team in business. While many of the concepts will appear simple, often the application into real life can be a little more challenging.

I know, deep down, that without the journey I have travelled, I would not have been able to have such a successful relationship or such a strong business. For every relationship, there will always be good days and not so good days, the trick is to make each good day better, and each not so good day less stressful.

My wonderful husband, William, supported me in writing this book so that I could share the secrets for building 'Dynamic Duos' for couples in business partnerships – ensuring that a couple's relationship and business thrive.

I hope this book gives you and your partner great insight into the key factors that will help guide you through the journey of life and business with each other.

INTRODUCTION

In every success story, you will find someone who has made a courageous decision.

PETER F. DRUCKER

What does it mean to be successful?

Everyone has a different version of this in their own mind. For some, it means having a great relationship, for others it may be having a nice house or plenty of money. Whatever the concept of success is in your own mind, this dream or vision of what you can strive towards motivates your actions, thoughts and behaviours in an effort to create the reality, from the fantasy.

For many couples, entering into a business journey together is driven by the vision that they can become successful. You never go into an experience deliberately for the pain, conflict, or for the stress it will create. Why would anyone knowingly purchase anything when they are only told the bad points or the faults?

Would you buy an airline ticket if you were told of all the possible things that could go wrong with the plane on your way to its destination? No, of course not. You buy an airline ticket so you can relax and enjoy the place you are bound for. You can sit on the beach in the sunshine, climb mountains, ski, explore, or visit loved ones at the other end.

The same is for business. If the only things you knew about starting a business were the potential failures, the risks and the arguments you would have with your partner, you would probably look at the opportunity and politely decline.

We all enter into business to fulfil a desire within ourselves – we enter with hopes, dreams and plans for being successful; however, often like the fairytales in life, we fall short of the fantasy that we thought was going to happen.

Whatever the reason for starting your business journey together, something has brought you to this point where you are reading this book in the hopes for some insight into how to keep your romance alive and grow a successful business together with your partner.

Clues that things are going wrong

There are tell-tale signs along the way that may be flashing some warning signs in your life, indicating that things are not as smooth as you would hope they would be. The relationship may be feeling a little dull or stagnant. Maybe you can't remember the last time you both had a lovely romantic evening together. Holidays are a distant wish, if only there was free time, or the money for that matter, to even take a few days off.

There seems to be more bickering over silly aspects that are really irrelevant in the grand scheme of things. Then there are the more obvious signs, such as words of anger about whose fault it is regarding a particular situation that both of you are facing. There may be hurtful comments, bitterness, and resentful feelings about the lack of equal efforts placed into the business or your relationship.

Whatever has brought you to this point – where you have decided to find some answers – it primarily means that there is still hope for both of you to bring your business and relationship back on track.

The beginning

For most couples in business, life starts out well, and then after a few years their conversations start to change, and they realise that their whole lives are focused solely around the business. It's as if there is nothing else to talk about together, and business problems are bulldozing their way through every area of their home life as well. Every waking moment is consumed with business problems, chatter or robust discussions on how to get out of a problem or situation, or who hasn't paid their account, or how can they pay the staff or meet this month's mortgage on their home.

The turning point comes when two people look at each other and find that they're just 'existing'. If you are starting to feel as if you just live with 'a work buddy', then you know things have to change.

In fact, I contacted a client and long-time friend recently and found out that after 38 years together, their relationship no longer held a magic spark. Their business was extremely successful, and from the outside they looked like the perfect couple, and yet, after all those years together they had gone their separate ways.

It is very important to maintain the excitement, mystery, romance and love throughout any life journey together, especially one that is carrying the extra pressure of running a business.

So how do we manage to do this?

What are those key factors and secrets that would make you that 'Dynamic Duo' together?

Universal laws

If you are to build a successful relationship and business with your partner, you have to follow some universal laws that are critically necessary to strengthen your foundations, both as individuals and as a couple.

There are certain 'laws', 'ingredients', or 'secrets' – if you want to call them that – to living successfully as individuals. Once you are aware and understand these, you can apply them to every aspect of your private and business life. The application of these 'laws' is about understanding the foundations and reasons behind why we do the things we do as human beings.

It all starts with the **WHY**.

If you look at our 'great' role models in society – men like Sir Richard Branson, Anthony Robbins, or amazing women like Oprah – you will see that they have 'deep purpose' in what they do. It is from this core motivation that the rest of their efforts in their business and in their lives make an enormous effect on the rest of the world.

If you look closely at this concept of 'purpose', there are important elements to it that you can apply to your own life and relationships. The reason I choose 'great' role models is to allow you to assimilate the principles I am to give and to align them with someone you acknowledge or recognise as successful or 'great'.

I will discuss the universal 'laws', and much more, within this book, and I hope that you find wisdom, enlightenment and a few tricks to help your relationship and business prosper.

SECTION ONE

Most people have attained
their greatest success one step
beyond their greatest failure.

Napoleon Hill

ESSENTIAL BASELINE

So how do you start from where you are at the moment?

Firstly, you have to establish a baseline of understanding about how the world works. Without an understanding of these universal laws to build upon a strong and solid foundation, it would be difficult to ensure the best is given by each of you into the relationship and your business.

Sure, there are plenty of couples in business who plough through the ups and downs, and weather the storms together, or maybe end up so exhausted with the battles on all fronts that they give up.

What if you could have the 'core elements' of the universal laws to make the 'Dynamic Duo' journey not only seem calm and effortless, but fruitful, rewarding, enjoyable, and successful for both of you?

For you to begin the journey of a thousand steps, you have to start by seeing the map of the road ahead.

This book provides the 'road map' for all successful couples in business, by discussing some core elements. If you need help with navigating the journey to becoming a 'Dynamic Duo', the following sections cover all the core elements and will help guide you.

I call these core elements the **Five Cs**.

The Five Cs

The **Five Cs** are five core elements that need to be understood and put into play when building successful relationships with your partner, while at the same time growing a successful business together.

Firstly, you must have **clarity** around who you are and where you are going in your own individual lives.

From there, you need to make a **commitment** to your partner and the business.

To enjoy any form of harmony throughout the journey, you must both learn effective **communication**, which will bring about greater understanding of each person's viewpoint and approach.

Once you have the foundations of a strong personal relationship with each other, only then can you combine your efforts to build a successful business through **cooperation.**

Finally, when each person within the relationship can work extremely well together as a team, you can begin to create your dreams and plans through **collaboration** towards the bigger goal.

Before launching into the Five Cs that create a 'Dynamic Duo' in business, I will give you a brief overview and explanation of how I see the world using five 'core living principles', which are essentially the 'foundations' of the Five Cs.

This will help you understand the reasons for setting the 'Dynamic Duo' pathway into the Five C components that will ensure you build a successful relationship and business partnership together.

The Five Core Living Principles

There are 'Five Core Living Principles' that form the foundations for life, which need to be established before setting out on the journey of building and renewing any relationship you have with your partner. These principles are more about seeing the 'bigger picture'.

You have to be able to know and learn about yourself and your partner in order to accept where things are currently sitting. Without accepting a starting point, like any journey, you cannot clearly define the pathway to your destination. These five core living principles are what will define your experiences in life, and these principles are the baseline for understanding the Five Cs.

1: What we focus on grows

You are probably aware of the fact that whatever you focus on grows. If you are focusing on buying a new car, you will suddenly see that type of car everywhere. It is not that they didn't exist before you started noticing them; it just means that now you are more aware of them because it has become a **focus** in your mind.

Therefore it stands to reason that if you focus on the negative things in your relationship, then that is what you will begin to see more of. Whereas, if you focus on the positive contributions that your partner offers to your relationship, then this will make for a much greater chance of survival in the years ahead.

I used to coach a client who approached her business as if everyone was out to rip her off. She would find and highlight all the customers who complained about her business, feeling they just wanted free stuff as compensation, and she'd justify her beliefs through the use of an exaggerated apportionment of blame.

I explained to her that customer feedback is great for a business, because it allows us to see where we can improve. If we leave holes inside our business and don't fix them up, exactly like a leaking bucket, eventually we won't have a business. My client shifted her perspective on things and now runs a thriving business. She takes care of every customer and appreciates them and their feedback, for without them, her family would have no income.

Whatever your situation is right now, I am positive there are areas that can be improved. Life and love is a journey – one that has ups and downs. There is no magic pill that will solve every problem overnight so that you never need to put in effort ever again.

You are, after all, human. The variety, mystery, challenges and joys bring about your definition of success, purely by the ability to survive and navigate your way through. To make your dreams and hopes a reality, or at least as closely reflected as possible in your everyday lives together, is what makes your journey purposeful.

2: Every human needs two things in life

After interviewing hundreds of people – and myriads of couples that are happy together, as well as those that are separating or divorcing – I found that every person wants (or needs) the same two things.

When asked what they most desire, beyond all the superficial, material or circumstantial desires, everyone arrives at the same conclusive two answers. Now, you may feel that this is a little simplistic, but if you ask that question often enough, you will find this to be a very common answer.

Firstly, we all seek to be 'happy'.

Now, 'happiness' will represent different things to different people at different times in their lives. For some it may be when they get a new car, or a new job. For others it may be when they finish their course, or when they get to enjoy Christmas holidays.

If you want to look more deeply at the concept of happiness, it could be described as inner peace, or love, self-worth or some embodiment of wholeness within ourselves.

Whatever the representation, if you can finally get to that point in the future where whatever you wanted has arrived, then this represents the ultimate prize, that great or 'heavenly' feeling of being 'happy'.

Secondly, we all want to 'learn and grow'.

At a core and fundamental level, we need to feel that we are progressing in our lives, and that we are better than we were the day before. This is why the human race strives for greater things, reaching into space, and testing all boundaries in order to evolve.

We can often feel that in times of stress, we are not moving forward. This can become frustrating for people, and therefore they may feel stuck or trapped in a situation or circumstance that is out of their control. The overwhelming feeling of not moving forward indicates that we are not learning or growing beyond this point. This can trigger unhappiness, so both components are required.

There are many different viewpoints as to what each person feels they need in life to be happy and successful. Regardless of what 'success' looks and feels like for you, there needs to be a great deal of happiness at the end of it all. You need to feel that you have achieved something worthwhile, conquered the fear, overcome the hurdles and put your best foot forward.

Take a few moments to ask yourself what you really, truly and deeply want, beyond anything else in this world. Make a list of the three things that would make you truly 'happy'.

And then write down three things that you feel you need to 'learn', in order to become the best version of yourself.

3: Everyone has a box of springs

The next important principle to understand is that everyone has 'baggage'. Some have more than others, but essentially, everyone carries the scars of life around with them.

So what is 'baggage' all about? Why do we have it, and how do we get rid of it?

Allow me to explain it like this . . .

Every experience, thought, object, emotion, person and belief is like a coiled spring. Each spring represents something in our lives that we have come across, and whether we like it or not, it becomes a part of us. Now imagine that every spring we collect goes into a box, and after 30 or so years, all those springs are now intricately entwined and building up pressure inside the box.

We can't simply open the box and pull out one spring because it is entangled with so many other things. That is why when we have an argument with our partner, all sorts of other, mostly irrelevant, topics come out in the middle of the discussion. One minute you may be discussing the priorities for next month's operations targets, and suddenly you are having a heated discussion about how the other person eats their porridge, or squeezes the toothpaste from the middle of the tube.

The only full and complete solution is to let your hand off the box. If you do this, you know that all of the springs will jump out of the box and land on the floor. For many people, especially those who are self-confessed 'control freaks' (myself included), this is a very scary process.

However, two great things happen when you let your hand off the lid of your box. Firstly, and most importantly, you have an 'empty' box. Secondly, you can choose what springs you want to put back into the box, if at all.

One spring may represent your mother-in-law, and another may be your pet. One spring may represent that horrible lamp that was given to you last Christmas, another may be a comment made in passing by a neighbour that irks you.

The great thing about shedding your excess 'baggage', or letting go of your box of springs, is that you allow yourselves the freedom to choose what you like and what you don't like. You can choose the things that you keep – the ones that are good for your soul and positive for your wellbeing. And you should carry no guilt about not keeping those springs that you simply do not want in your life any more.

It is a very liberating experience!

It also brings greater perspective about the things that truly matter in life.

If you have not yet tried this process, feel free to let go of everything that is weighing you down – emotionally, mentally, physically and spiritually – in life. Take a few hours for yourself and find a quiet space, free of distraction or disruption. Let your hand off your box of springs. And remind yourself that you cannot control anything! The only thing that was ever in your control was yourself. Be free of guilt, be free of fear, be gentle on yourself and know that everything will be okay.

4: Everyone has a different view

One of the greatest causes of an argument with another person, is your differing points of view. We see it all the time in business and in relationships, where one person believes that they are right and the other person is wrong. This causes untold pain and stress between two people. Not only is the argument generally due to their difference of opinion, it is also due to the fact that each person is trying to get the other person to agree with them.

Sometimes we can become angry with our partner when they do not adopt or agree with what we believe. After all, our purpose is to get our point across and have an agreement that what we are saying is correct, and it's the truth.

Perspectives and opinions are similar to watching an accident in the middle of an intersection. Each person stands on a different corner, which means each person has a different viewpoint, and yet they all see the same accident. If a police officer interviewed each person, there would be slightly different versions of the same event. One person may blame the cat that ran across the road, while the person on the opposite corner will swear that there was no cat.

The question is, who is telling the truth?

And the answer is that they **all** are.

People will tell their version of events as they see it. The key to fully understanding any given situation is to make sure we speak with every person at the scene and not take any one person's statement or perspective as the complete picture.

What does this have to do with our relationships and our business?

You and your partner will each have different views on how your business should run, what your relationship should have or reflect, who you should or should not employ, and a million other options for every decision that you could possibly come up with during the course of your journey together. You can't foresee everything; however, you can ensure that you are aware of the different corners of the intersection.

Let go of the emotion, let go of judgement and stick to the facts. Remain emotionally neutral when reviewing the viewpoints around the intersection.

In your lives and business together, a 'Dynamic Duo' couple must remove themselves from their own corner and review the situation from all angles. And they must take logic, reasoning and different viewpoints into consideration.

If both people in a partnership understand that no **one** person is totally correct by standing firm on their own statement, consideration of all angles will bring about better perspectives for all.

5: The law of balance

The fifth core living principle for a successful life is the understanding of the 'law of balance'[1]. We all know about Sir Isaac Newton, who sat underneath the apple tree and the apple fell and hit him on the head.

---

[1] Millman, D 1995,*The Laws of the Spirit: A Tale of Transformation*, HJ Kramer and New World Library, California, USA.

From that he devised the 'law of gravity'. Even though we cannot see gravity, we know and can feel its effect. The same thing happens with 'balance'.

If you have ever seen a big, old grandfather clock, you will notice a pendulum swinging from side to side that keeps time ticking away. Tick . . . Tock . . . Tick . . . Tock . . . Watching the clock ticking away, you will notice that whatever distance the pendulum is pulled in one direction, the motion of the arc will swing to the exact distance on the opposite side. Why, because of the law of balance. It states that to remain in equilibrium, the forces must be *equal* and *opposite* distance from the centre.

So how does this relate to a couple in business together, trying to balance their romantic life, children, work schedules and private life? The more one person tries to pull in one direction, the partner has to pull in the opposite direction in order to maintain balance.

Now, you may be thinking about those men that work extremely long hours, and their wives who demand that they spend more time at home with the family. This is a perfect example of a couple trying to maintain balance. The longer he works, the more demanding she becomes. Remember, the pressure applied to the pendulum has to be equal and opposite to maintain balance.

There may be times when things get completely out of balance, for example, if both people are working too much, and neither of them have enough rest or family time. In these cases, there may be another cause that will force itself into the mix to ensure balance is restored. This could be a serious health issue, relationship breakdown, or a mechanical failure that forces work to halt. Something has to give somewhere along the line – it is just the way things go. Just like we cannot stop gravity, balance will take its fee when the time comes.

Now that I have covered off the basic 'foundations' to living, you can begin to enrich your relationships and your business with the Five Cs – the five components that will build stronger connections between you and your partner, and ultimately set your business up for success.

SECTION TWO

What lies behind you and what lies in front of you, pales in comparison to what lies inside of you.

Ralph Waldo Emerson

CLARITY

Before any journey begins, you need to be clear about where you are going. Not only do you need to know your destination, but you also need a starting point before you can begin the journey. Having both lets you know how long it will take to get there and the general direction you need to be going in order to reach the destination in a somewhat timely and efficient manner. You need complete clarity about the journey ahead.

If you have ever taken a long journey to a place you have never been, then you would probably refer to a map. Some of you may be thinking to just use a GPS; however, even they have limitations. For example, a GPS will take you to the destination that you input, but it won't give you the entire landscape or tell you the most efficient way of covering multiple destinations.

A few years ago, while I was working for a large franchise organisation as their Territory Manager, I was required to visit 17 stores in Townsville. I had never been to Townsville before, and while the GPS could take me to each store individually, I needed the entire map to show me the layout of all the suburbs. I then planned the stores in a specific order so that I was not doubling back on my journey. And I created a logical and efficient circular route that covered every store in a sequence.

Truly contented people have one core thing in common, they know themselves deeply. They have clarity around who they are and where they fit into the world around them. They see the entire landscape and know the multitude of amazing destinations that surround them. Successful people have clear visions of their goals and their future.

To get yourself into a clear frame of mind, you need to begin by asking yourself – and your partner – some pretty important questions. So let's look more closely at what these questions are.

Who are you as an individual?

Who are you as a person? Where have you come from, and where are you going in your life? What defines who you are? What makes you happy?

If you look at highly effective and successful people, they are very content within themselves. They know who they are as individuals. They understand their place in the world, and they know what their purpose for living is.

So the question is, did they become successful before they knew about themselves, or did they know who they were first, and this is what led them to that success?

Regardless of what came first, you can start to find clarity at whatever stage of success you are by taking a few moments with yourself and looking in the mirror.

What do you see? Do you even like the person staring back at you?

Acceptance of yourself as a human being, with all of your faults and mistakes, is the greatest step you can make in becoming a content and successful individual. Without accepting who you are in the very beginning, you would constantly be running and hiding from that person you saw in the mirror. You would shy away from your responsibilities, hide from all your failings or mistakes, and you would deny your desires, wants, and your basic right to live a long and fruitful life.

Acceptance of yourself is the foundation to being accepted by others. It seems simple enough, and yet many people carry guilt, fear and regret around with them every day, and it impacts upon their ability to make great business and life-changing decisions that will benefit themselves and their families.

Let's take it one step further now – can you look in the mirror and honestly say that you **love** who you are?

Again, if you can't love your own self, how can you possibly believe that anyone else loves you? It would be a contradiction to your own beliefs, and the very thought of this could cause you to reject the love that someone else may have to offer you, because you don't feel love for yourself.

Here is a little secret – everyone makes mistakes. Every person on the face of the earth has done something that they are ashamed of, or feel bad or embarrassed about. The way someone overcomes this is through accepting that they are only human and forgiving themselves for whatever it is, as well as letting go of the emotional baggage that comes along with that process.

Your first step in becoming successful within your relationships and business is in knowing and loving who you are today. With this process comes the freedom to be yourself, and to not make any apologies for being you. It is not only liberating but it also allows for you to then become fluid, adapting, changing and evolving as you learn and grow through the journey of life.

Allow yourself to be aligned within your head and your heart. Make sure that both your head and your heart are truthful and congruent to each other. Being truthful to yourself about what you want is the best way to alleviate internal stress and frustrations, as you attempt to be authentic yet still keep other people happy.

Who are you as a couple?

Once you have established yourself as your own person, with all your own individual desires in life, you can then begin to share that life with someone else – a partner, lover, or spouse. The person you are in partnership with is with you for a reason. You are sharing a part of yourself with them – so too, they are with you. You both need to be gaining something from the relationship, otherwise, why would you be together, right?

My first relationship and marriage lasted 14 years, and two children, so there must have been something good there to start with. We were great friends as teenagers. And when it all came down to it, who else would I marry but my best friend? He loved me at a time in my life when I felt most unlovable, but ultimately this love was not strong enough to keep us together, and eventually I only felt a type of brotherly love for him.

With my second husband, I was older and wiser, plus I had done a lot of soul-searching within myself and knew my non-negotiables – what I was not prepared to compromise on. When we met, it was as if we had been searching our whole lives for each other. The depth of love and commitment we still have to this day seems eternal, and there is no other goal more important to us than to spend the rest of our lives growing together, learning from and supporting each other.

Couples need to have clarity around why they are together. Remember the two things that every human being needs – to be happy and to learn and grow. There is no doubt that when you join with another person in a relationship, you join with them to seek happiness in the form of love – love that your partner receives from you, and love that your partner returns to you.

It is absolutely amazing when that love is equally given and received by both people. Sometimes, one person finds they are giving more than they feel they are receiving from their partner, and this is where things can sometimes feel a little out of balance. Remember, balance is also an important part of building a successful relationship and business together.

What is your purpose together?

I believe that people come together for a reason. They learn about each other, as well as learn about themselves in the process of experiencing moments in life together. Nothing is greater as a challenging force, than when two people join together as a 'couple'.

Being in a relationship can challenge you to the very core of who you are, and some people like what they see, while others do not. Therefore they struggle to accept or adjust themselves in accordance with the relationship's needs. Finding the reason or purpose for you being together as a couple means understanding what you are meant to be learning from and sharing with each other along the way.

Sometimes the reason for learning is not always clear. For example, my ex-husband showed me love by being jealous, or possessive, which was not 'love', and yet I learnt much about who I am as a person through this very realisation. This was not actually the type of love that was healthy for a couple's relationship or business. And as a result, I learnt what to look for in any future partner, and what type of relationship *was* healthy and fulfilling.

Before you form any relationship, you are an individual first.

As individuals, you have set yourself some goals that you aim to achieve in life. Maybe this started when you were much younger. For example, at the age of 13, my eldest daughter decided that she want to join the Air Force as a pilot.

I too had that dream when I was a teenager; however, my life never quite turned out how I had imagined it. So when it came to supporting my daughter with her career choice, I supported her as much as I possibly could, and now she is achieving that dream and graduating as a pilot, training in the Air Force, as I write this book. Her partner is the most supportive person I could ever imagine for her career, which makes her success much easier to achieve.

In many ways, I regret not having that support from my parents, or my ex-husband, to help me achieve my dreams or goals. Maybe this created problems in our marriage, long before the cracks really started to show, and the marriage became irreversibly damaged because of this.

Currently, William and I now know that our relationship is for life. Our purpose together is to live out our lives, loving and supporting each other. We both want to grow old together, live and enjoy every moment. We both want to build a successful business, and we openly share these common visions of our purpose and reasons for being together in a relationship.

Find out your purpose together, and find the reason why you are both in the relationship. What are you both gaining from each other by being together? Have discussions around what you are hoping to achieve in sharing your lives together. The more you both talk about things, the clearer your future will be together.

Is there imbalance in your love?

When your partner says 'I love you', how do you feel? Does it make you feel warm and fuzzy, or are you a little sceptical on the genuine feeling behind those words? Maybe you are feeling there is some imbalance in the relationship, and yet you can't quite put your finger on what is going wrong or the aspect that may be missing.

Through years of observation, I have noticed that different people express their love at different times, in a variety of ways, and behaviours do not always fully convey the true depth of someone's capacity to give and receive love. Various cultures have different approaches to showing affection, to which some may mistake as being distant, or not 'in love' with their partner or spouse. I believe much of this comes down to a person's ability, attitude and capacity for love.

Imagine that the flow of love between two people is like pouring water. If one person has a jug of water to give, but the other person only has a cup. How much love can the person receiving carry? That's right, only as much as the cup can hold.

If the person giving love keeps pouring from their jug, once their partner's cup is full, then the excess will fall to the ground and be wasted. The effect then between couples in this type of situation can be seen as smothering or over-bearing for the person whose cup is full and now overflowing. So too, the person giving from their cup will end up with providing nothing significant in their partner's jug, which can leave them feeling empty.

Each person within the relationship can help their partner feel safe, loved, comfortable and valued through words and actions that will bring about a growing strength between them.

Each person can stretch their capacity to give and receive love if they choose to. Growing in love can expand a person's capacity, like exchanging a cup for a beaker, a beaker for a pint, a pint for a jug.

Each person can slowly increase their capacity to feel, give and receive love for each other through intimate actions, words, and sharing their feelings and thoughts with their partner. This takes practice, patience and a lot of commitment from each person in the relationship.

Having clarity around each person's ability and capacity to love the other person will greatly identify any gaps where one person is left feeling unfulfilled, or the other person is feeling smothered or drowned in 'love'.

So how do couples ensure they can fulfil each other's needs when it comes to being in love and sharing their quality time together? How do they embrace their depth of love equally together?

The answers will always come back to how much one person can love themselves. The deeper they can feel true love for their own self will ensure they know their own self-worth and never feel insecure or worthless in any relationship.

How do you differ from one another?

They say that opposites attract, and generally you admire in others the things you feel lacking in yourself. So how does this work in couples? You each have different personalities – there are those who are very sociable and those who are extremely shy.

Some prefer being in control, while others lack the desire to take the lead role. Maybe you see things more abstractly, such as being more impressionistic and creative, while your partner is more technical and logical. Whatever the belief, there are reasons why two people's personalities and characteristics complement each other's strengths and weaknesses.

Being clear on your own strengths and weaknesses will help you acknowledge the strengths and weaknesses within your partner. This is not designed to highlight each other's weaknesses as a tool to use for the 'art of war' in the bedroom. It is more to understand and appreciate how each person contributes to the relationship. Perhaps your personality strengths fill in for your partner's weaknesses, and vice versa. Learning to appreciate how you are different allows each couple to give thanks for the other person's abilities.

Remember that what you focus on becomes top of mind in your awareness. It is imperative that you focus on our partner's strengths and lift them up, bringing their gifts to the forefront of your communication with them.

It's never constructive to run your partner down for their weaknesses, as we are all human, and we all have our limitations in certain areas. Highlight where your partner has done well. Thank them for their efforts, even if they fall short of your own expectations. By building support around each other's strengths, you actually magnify them, increasing each person's motivation, confidence, and subsequently their ability to do each task becomes better with practise.

To understand 'behaviours' and how each person approaches life, we have enclosed an overview of different personalities in the next few pages to show the strengths and weaknesses of each personality style. We have also included some information as to how you can recognise signs of stress and how to best communicate effectively with each personality type.

Let's firstly look at the different personality types. These personalities are based on the Wilson learning platform[2].

---

[2] Wilson Learning Social Styles, Building Relationship Versatility, viewed 28 August 2018, <https://www.wilsonlearning.com/wlw/products/brv>.

How to identify personalities by their behaviours

DRIVER
They walk ahead of other people.
They talk abruptly.
They seem angry all the time.
They are the first ones to finish their dinner.
There are task orientated.
They are serious.

EXPRESSIVE
They wear colourful clothes.
They are loud.
They are social.
They laugh a lot.
They are the last ones to finish dinner (due to talking).
They wear bright makeup.

ANALYTICAL
They are quiet and reserved.
They don't like to be the centre of attention or be put on the spot.
They hide behind the scenes.
They wear formal clothing.
They are neat and tidy.
They pick at their food.
They have a fussy behaviour.

AMIABLE
They are smiling and friendly.
They share anything they have with others (including food).
The wear comfortable and casual clothing.
The have an easy-going attitude towards anything.
They are willing to help anyone at any time.
They are most likely in the kitchen cleaning up after a party.

Strengths and weaknesses

DRIVER

Strengths

Control	Forward	Serious
Efficient	Hardworking	Self-driven
Determined	Dependable	Courageous
Fast decision-maker	Motivated	

Weaknesses

Dominant	Unkind	Rough
Autocratic	None diplomatic	Bossy
Harsh	Pushy	Impatient
Impulsive	Uncompromising	Quick tempered

Key attributes

Drivers are usually fast and efficient hardworkers. They get on with the job and don't waste time. They are quick at making decisions and are very good at controlling, supervising and managing others.

Most compatible with: Amiable

Strengths and weaknesses *continued*

EXPRESSIVE

Strengths

Good motivator	Colourful	Exciting
Inspirational	Artistic	Outgoing
Dynamic	Dreamers	Courageous
Flamboyant	Influential	

Weaknesses

Impulsive	Dramatic	Careless
Selfish	Emotional	Impatient
Self-centred	Thoughtless	Quick tempered
Pushy	Unrealistic	

Key attributes

Expressive people are the best public speakers, and they are very influential and motivational. They are good coaches, teachers, politicians, actors, lawyers and trainers.

Most compatible with: Analytical

Strengths and weaknesses *continued*

ANALYTICAL

Strengths

Technical	Articulate	Skilful
Cautious	Accurate	Strategic
Detailed	Precise	

Weaknesses

Cunning	Indecisive	Unemotional
Uncompromising	Resistant to change	Inconsiderate
Fussy	Unkind	

Key attributes

Analytical people are very detailed and accurate with what they do. They are very good at planning and calculating. They are good doctors, engineers, accountants and technicians.

Most compatible with: Expressive

Strengths and weaknesses *continued*

AMIABLE

Strengths

Kind	Dependable	Compassionate
Courteous	Friendly	Patient
Agreeable	Understanding	Trustworthy
Helpful	Emotional	
Loyal	Considerate	

Weaknesses

Laid back	Lacks drive	Doormat
Lazy	Too casual	Unassertive
Unmotivated	Indecisive	

Key attributes

Amiable people are compassionate, helpful, friendly, kind and courteous. They are good with children, and are good doctors, psychologists, nurses, teachers, and they work well in sales and marketing.

Most compatible with: Driver

During an argument keep these things in mind

DRIVER

Best way to communicate

Give straight and direct, honest answers.

Get to the point quickly.

State the facts.

Ask them for help.

Allow them to be the authority.

Give genuine positive support and assistance.

Apologise immediately if you make a mistake.

Worst way to communicate

Hide things from them.

Give incorrect information.

Fluff around with answers that don't say anything or are not relevant.

Fob them off.

Being the 'yes' person.

Not taking them seriously.

During an argument keep these things in mind *continued*

EXPRESSIVE

Best way to communicate

Show excitement.
State what's in it for them.
Flatter them and say wonderful things about them.
Support their ideas and follow their lead.
Let them be the centre of attention.
Let them come up with the ideas.
Don't jump on every single idea, let them mull over it for a while.

Worst way to communicate

Ignore them.
Damage their ego or hurt their pride.
Steal their thunder.
Talk over them.
Take away their limelight.
Place another person above them in priority or favour someone else.

During an argument keep these things in mind *continued*

ANALYTICAL

Best way to communicate

Give them heaps of clear and concise information.

Allow them plenty of thinking time.

Give them accurate and detailed facts.

Don't push or hurry them for an answer.

Don't yell, as they may withdraw away from conflict.

Worst way to communicate

Expecting decisions in a rushed or pressured situation.

Lack of detail, substance or forethought.

Inaccurate information.

Too much emotional overflow.

Putting them on the spot in front of others.

Ganging up with someone else to highlight their mistakes.

Highlighting their mistakes at all.

Applying blame to something they have done.

During an argument keep these things in mind *continued*

AMIABLE

Best way to communicate

Give courteous and polite requests.
Ask for help with something.
Give clear instructions for what you want done.
Follow up with them.
Allow them time for processing information.
Be firm and fair.
Appeal to their gentle nature by being gentle in your approach.

Worst way to communicate

Using pushy or bullying tactics.
Don't lie to them or abuse their loyalty.
Don't be mean or nasty about them as a person.
Don't betray their trust.

What is your role in the relationship?

Understanding yourself and your partner is the first step in building a stronger relationship. Without knowing your own purpose and that of the other person, you cannot begin to appreciate each other, or accept each other's shortcomings, especially once you have already acknowledged your own shortcomings. Once you identify your own personality, you can look at how it complements your partner's personality.

To then build upon your relationship, understanding each other's 'Love Language' helps you to recognise the best way to demonstrate and express your love for each other in different ways.

There is a book by Gary Chapman that talks about the 'Five Love Languages', and how couples can express their heartfelt commitment to each other. It also allows couples to openly discuss what language they best receive as well. It is a book well worth reading if you are feeling that the style of communication between you and your partner is not as effective as it should be.

The 'Five Love Languages' are:
- Words of affirmation
- Acts of service
- Receiving gifts
- Quality time
- Physical touch[3]

---

3 Chapman, G 2010, *The Five Love Languages*, Northfield Publishing, Chicago, USA.

Often we don't even recognise the efforts of our partner whenever they are attempting to express their love. Maybe it's like being in a house where one person only speaks Spanish, while the other person only speaks Chinese. Both can understand themselves, but not the other person.

In relationships, your partner may not fully understand what it is that you need to receive in order to feel or recognise the fact that they love you. They may say 'I love you' all the time; however, they never help around the house, and yet some individuals feel that helping out is a form of saying 'I love you'.

Some individuals are more affectionate than others and require intimacy or physical touch to express love, and yet the partner does the dishes, works hard and spends their spare time in the garage tinkering around, thinking that they are building something for their family. The very fact that they do not recognise that their partner needs intimate touch or quality time together may mean that they are placing effort in the wrong area of the relationship according to their partner. The romance, therefore, may fizzle out, the daily routine becomes tiresome and stagnant, and the person needing intimacy may just go looking for it somewhere else. And that is a disaster.

Being aware of each other's receptiveness is so important, as this tells you where effort is required when it comes to building and strengthening the relationship. Whatever happens within your relationship, the 'Love Languages' is something that you need to discover about each other. Maybe your partner needs affirmation or encouragement to feel the love and romance between you. It may be more acts of service, or words of endearment, or maybe intimate touch will confirm your love for them. Talk things through and learn about each other's likes and dislikes.

It doesn't all have to match up now, but it certainly helps when you are trying to piece together why your arguments come about in the first place, or how to reduce the conflict during times of stress.

The power of success or destruction lies in your hands. Only you have the power to turn things around before it is too late in your relationship. Start by opening up about yourself. Once you know who you are and what you like best, you can explain these things to your partner.

Find out what makes them happy, how they feel, what their needs in the relationship are. Talk through what annoys you both when trying to show love, and describe why it bothers you. All these things will lead you both to greater understanding about your commitment to each other and how best to communicate together.

What is your role in the business?

Now that we have discussed you both as individuals, your purpose together as a couple, your different strengths and weaknesses, and what your role is within the relationship, we can begin to discuss the role each of you plays within the business.

Whatever discussions occur between you and your partner, you will need to be mindful of the difference between your expectations and reality. With hope, there will be at least one person in the relationship that has a good sense of business understanding, skills and acumen.

You both must allow yourselves the freedom to be who each of you are. If there is continual pressure to behave a certain way, then it can lead to built-up resentment or frustration for both the receiver and the dictator of how and what you can and can't do or be. Stifling each other's self-expression can also create more disharmonies within the relationship.

Instead, it's better to bring the best version of yourself into the business and the relationship as much as possible.

Understanding that you are each different and have different approaches to life helps you to become more tolerant of the self-expression and the freedom of unconditional love in your relationship and business.

So let's look at the variety of roles within a business so that you can gain a better understanding of what best suits you and your partner, as this will ultimately give you insight into what will ensure your business grows and flourishes.

The variety of roles

Normally there will be one person to take the lead, make decisions and speak up about the direction that is to be taken, while the complementing partner will support, follow, and cooperate with whatever task needs to be completed. Both people in each of these roles are just as important as the other.

Without support, a leader will achieve nothing. A leader can successfully give orders, but there will be no one carrying them out. Similarly, without direction, an amiable or quiet person will sit and wait for someone to advise them what to do next. They often cannot see the bigger picture in order to achieve significant ground-breaking goals, without the guidance and direction from the leader. In effect, both people need each other to assist them in different ways.

If one partner is more creative and has a more entrepreneurial spirit, then they will have a burning desire to be in business for themselves. Often the other person is not as entrepreneurial. They may give into the decision of starting a business together reluctantly, and so the journey begins sometimes with resistance, doubt and conflict between them.

Generally an analytical person will be cautious, cynical, and negative towards any brilliantly creative and impulsive idea that the entrepreneur has generated, knowing that within a couple of weeks all will be dropped by the wayside as it becomes too difficult, or the next new, shiny bright idea has come along, taking all the entrepreneur's attention.

Some of you reading this may be giggling, having seen this happen to someone else. Those experiencing it at the moment in their own relationship probably won't be laughing, as they will be either very frustrated or crying by now.

The essence of understanding what your personality types are gives greater insight into how and why the rollercoaster of business affects everyone differently. Some are visionaries with their head in the clouds, while others are the labourers with their feet planted firmly on the ground. Any successful business needs both.

In fact, one of the most highly recommended books about business is *The EMyth* by Michael Gerber. He describes the three different roles needed within a business or in a solo operation. They are the 'technician', the 'manager', and the 'entrepreneur'[4].

He further explains that couples who work together within a business can share the load, at least each wearing one of the three hats required, thereby filling two places within the business. Working together in trust, love and combined efforts helps to build a successful business together.

---

4   Gerber M E 2009, *The EMyth Revisited, Why most small businesses don't work and what to do about it*, Harper Collins Publishers, USA.

So have a close look at your business's needs, and your own strengths and the strengths of your partner. You need to then clearly identify and communicate with your partner what each person will do within the business and at home.

One of you may be great at administration, while the other is the more technical. One may be the visionary, while the other is great at managing others to carry out the work required, or one keeps the family home in order.

Whatever your skill set, each of you has something of value to contribute to the business function, as well as to the relationship at home. Supporting each other is the key.

So don't be too hard on each other or yourself, as you are both human and experience ups and downs. Be realistic with the expectations you place on each other and yourself to ensure that there is still plenty of time to relax and enjoy the other side to life, which is to love each other at the end of a long and busy day.

Remember to stop, look at each other, smile and appreciate each person's contribution to the partnership. And always find positive ways to support the efforts and the roles each person plays.

SECTION THREE

The best and most beautiful things
in this world cannot be seen or even
heard, but must be felt with the heart.

Helen Keller

COMMITMENT

Now that you know who you are, and who your partner is – for all their good points and bad points – you can start working through your relationship commitments to one another to build a strong foundation for growing your business together.

In order to do this, it is imperative that you think back to why you made this relationship commitment to each other in the first place. Look at what you want to achieve together in your relationship. Look at why you fell in love and focus on the romance and 'spark' within your relationships, for this passion forms the basis of a successful business together.

There is no other naturally and biologically initiated euphoric feeling on the planet like falling in love. Your emotions take control when you begin dating, and that giddy excitement and warm fuzzy feeling flows through both of you, and then you realise that you are in love.

During the early stages of a relationship, you both overlook the little things – shortcomings and the failings in your potential 'soul mate' – and instead you focus purely on each other's glowing qualities.

The purpose of focusing on the feelings you experienced when you first met your partner is to reconnect the strong emotions you felt and draw to the forefront the reasons you came together in the first place, as something must have been 'igniting' between you.

Some of you may be thinking, *but those are the very things that drive me nuts now*. If this is the case, then this is a good place to be, because it highlights some critical adjustments that you may need to make within yourself in order to clear the barriers towards building your successful relationship and business together.

When couples form a commitment for their personal relationship, their love sparks a fantastic vision for their future. Sometimes that vision includes having children together, other times there is a wonderful vision of running a business together and building something up to make a lot of money, living a wonderful lifestyle and retiring together at the ripe old age of thirty-five. For some couples, the vision includes both children and business.

Commitment can also be about understanding what motivates each person in the relationship, as well as being tolerant and compassionate of our humanness, and knowing without a shadow of doubt that your partner is supporting you at all times. It's about building respect for each other despite your differences. Commitment relies upon entrusting one another with your heart and soul, and with the money too, of course. The depth of commitment becomes stronger between two people who are honest and transparent with each other, and the relationship becomes more fulfilling for both of you.

Take some time to analyse your current relationship status. What do you feel is lacking or missing in the romance and love you share?

Attitude and ability

Whenever people make a commitment, whether in a personal relationship or a business dealing, there are two aspects that need to combine in order to bring about a successful partnership – having the right attitude and following through with the required ability.

The first critical component to a successful 'Dynamic Duo' comes down to each person's 'attitude'. Are you both willing to do whatever it takes to make the partnership work? Is one partner just in the relationship for themselves? Or, are you working together so that both parties can succeed in the situation?

Attitude plays an important part when it comes down to the moral and ethical transactions that will need to happen between two people at the critical moments.

Times of stress, immense pressure, mistakes and shortfalls can all bring out the devil in each person. Those who have a genuine intent and care to see a win/win situation for everyone are the types of people who have the right attitude for romantic partnerships and business relationships.

The second component is the 'ability' to keep the commitment made between each other in the relationship. While a person may have an attitude of wanting to make things work, their ability to actually pull it off may need some extra work. This could be in the area of increasing skills, social awareness, communication and teamwork.

Understanding compatibility and acceptance

Being compatible does not mean that you have to spend every waking moment together. It means that you need to understand and respect each other's differences, as well as where you fit and work together to complement each other's skills.

Some people like to have space, while others prefer to be more social. Some like to put great efforts into their work and hobbies, while others are homebodies and love to spend time with their partner and family members. Every person has different priorities at different times, which can sometimes be out of sync with the other person.

Have you ever tried being romantic while your partner is working on the car? Most likely he will probably tell you to bugger off. Distract a woman while she is cooking, and you may get a frying pan spatula across the knuckles. We each have different times, different cycles, different things going on in our minds every second of the day.

Understanding individuality and togetherness

You both need time apart to spend time alone for self-reflection, and you also need time together – time for work, romance, and communication. It is all about that wonderful 'law of balance'.

Make plans to spend time romantically together (i.e. arrange a 'date night'), as this will allow you to both coincide your schedules. You will then know that this is how the time is to be spent – so you can make an effort, buy her some flowers, or put on that extra special perfume that you know he likes. Setting this time aside as a priority will indicate your attitude towards building a strong and deeply loving relationship with your partner.

Conversely, having separate space while working hard alongside each other is all about acceptance of your differences and finding ways to make things work together. The wellbeing of your relationship – both in and out of work time – comes down to a very simple yet often under-valued thing called 'quality communication'. Talk to each other, check in with your partner, understand and communicate on when is 'together time' and when is 'alone time'.

Compatibility is about understanding and accepting your own strengths and weaknesses, as well as appreciating the strengths and weaknesses in your partner. Allowance and tolerance of each other goes hand in hand with relationships. There will be things that will annoy the absolute daylights out of you about your partner. But that is who they are, and you have to accept them for *all* they are and not try to change them.

The only person who can change someone is themselves. They have to recognise something within themselves that they do not like, and they must want to change that about themselves. No one can change someone else.

However, what we can do is learn from each other. What *is* in our control is how we react to our partner's behaviours and actions. By them naturally being who they are, this is teaching us something about who we are and what we need to learn about ourselves.

When two people fall in love, it is usually due to some qualities that we see in the other person that we lack within ourselves. I am shy, so I rely on my husband to be the socialiser for the both of us. I get stressed, so my partner is my calming influence. He has his head in the clouds, and I am the more grounding person in our relationship. While there may be some great ideas he comes up with, I can bring forward many reasons why something may not work as well as initially thought. This balance helps us both to support each other in making good business and life decisions together.

That is how we can be compatible to each other.

If you look around at couples, you may see one person who is very loud, while the other is soft and gentle. One person may be colourful and chatty, while the other is sombre and quiet. These people can learn from each other. The chatty person can learn to mellow a little, while the sombre person can learn to become brighter and more engaging. The balance of each person is highlighted by the great differences between two people within a relationship. For example, the greater the anger in one, the more you will find compassion in the other.

Applying balance and acceptance

Compatibility is there to maintain the balance in the relationship. This is great for a business relationship as well because it allows for one person to take on the 'sales and marketing' role, while the other takes on the 'operations and logistics' role. One person becomes the front end or 'face' of the business, while the other person makes everything happen in the background. Without either one or the other, the business would fall apart.

Identify your compatible roles within your relationship and your business. Write down what parts you can play more effectively to ensure that every aspect is covered within the business and your relationship. Who will lead the business aspect and who will lead the romantic aspect of your relationship together?

Acceptance of each other's differences and how that contributes to a successful partnership is the key to letting go of the frustrations and resentments that build up between two people when their expectations of what they believe 'should and should not happen' are not met.

Combining your visions and values

Where a couple definitely does need to be compatible is in their 'moral compass'. Each person's beliefs, core values, and the visions that they have for their future must be generally well aligned. If you are not on the same page as a couple, whether it be with parenting, or business decisions, then eventually the rift between two people grows and problems or differences may become insurmountable.

Importantly, couples who work together will need to identify where your visions and values lie together. If one person seeks immense wealth, while the other is happy just making enough to live, then it will begin to show in the stressful times during which each couple faces the choices that will determine your future together.

Compatibility is about being in agreement for the overall objectives that you wish to set out for your lives together. It comes down to your core values and knowing that your partner values the same things as you do. Work together to find a happy and harmonious choice – one that satisfies both of your dreams, and integrity, as well as complements your individual skillsets.

Harmony within a relationship is great. There is a sense of contentment, as two people look towards each other at the end of the day and feel comfort in that they are on the same page together. If you look long enough at each other during these contented moments, you will find yourself smiling together. This is a good thing, and most loving couples will embrace each other at this point. Even if they have had a busy or tough day, once the air is clear and they are able to resolve any differences together relatively easily, the next thing is to kiss and make up.

Bringing your visions together encourages each of you to remove the barriers of work and bring your personal loving and romantic relationship to the forefront. So take the time to sit together and bring about harmony in your vision for your future together. Look each other in the eyes when you say cheers and congratulate each other on working something out together. Celebrate with pride that you are able to dream big together, as this will bring out the magic spark of intimacy that every couple needs to thrive.

Love and intimacy

Remember when you first met, there was probably a lot of passion between you. Being in love draws two people together with a strong attraction and desire for intimacy. It often becomes the gauge through which two people measure how 'in love' they are, and yet this is only a part of the full level of required commitment between two people.

Often the spark in a romantic relationship starts to fade a little after the honeymoon phase is over. The routine of life sets in and the roundabout of living, eating, working and sleeping sets in. It is during this phase that the alternative aspects of commitment take over.

These are the ethical conditions of promises, loyalty, effort, sacrifice and friendship. These aspects of your relationship then carry the commitment level when the romantic spark or chemistry is fizzling out.

When couples run a business together, they find that over time there is less intimacy, with both partners often going to bed too exhausted to be romantic, and then they wake up to start work all over again. It is during these times that individuals begin to question the relationship value and strength between them.

If this is the case, the impact of questioning the 'commitment' needs to be addressed immediately. The level of love and intimacy that both partners will seek and desire can often be at different levels. Whether it is because of your differing personalities, or the fact that you have lots of environmental stress, or you are a female and your partner is a man.

Whatever is creating the gap of intimacy between you both, it is imperative to address things in order for you to cement your commitment within your relationship, which can then overflow into your business life together.

But how do you do this?

Let me guide you through some of the aspects that might need to be addressed, and how you can work on these for the benefit of both your personal and business relationships.

The art of loving a woman

Men – it is important that your woman knows that she is special, beautiful, worthy and precious to you. And sometimes, you don't even need words to express these things! In fact, sometimes she might just want you to take her up in your arms and sweep her lovingly off her feet (literally or figuratively). You will feel masculine, and she will feel feminine. It can be a beautiful union between two people.

Drink in the magnificence of each other's skin, and walk through the process of taking things slowly. Shut out the world and celebrate the passionate part of intimacy, romance, and block out anything that threatens to break the focus from each other in those moments.

Make it your hobby to learn the art of making love to your woman. Find out her desires, seek out her pleasures, take her over the mountain of ecstasy and bring her down again with all the strength and power that only a man can possess, as he leads the dance between the union and partnership of lovemaking.

I believe that almost every female should be able to experience and enjoy an orgasm like men can. It can provide great internal stress relief and a new lease on her life, as well as greater enjoyment for both of you in the bedroom. For a woman to achieve this, a great level of trust has to be present between you both. She needs to trust her partner implicitly in order to relax enough and let go of all inhibitions, fears, overwhelming thoughts and daily activities plaguing her mind.

The trouble is that many women don't know how to achieve this, and many men can't find the 'right buttons' to push either. Guys probably give up because it is like trying to see 'God'. It is almost an unchartered part of the universe, and sometimes it takes too long to get there, so the journey stops, or in most cases, never begins. 'Intimacy' for the couple in business together can at times be another 'chore'. It takes about three minutes, if you are lucky, and then life gets back to 'normal', whatever that is.

The art of loving a man

To love a man is very different to loving a woman. Men have different views on life, different priorities and motivators, and sometimes this is a challenge for women to truly understand what to do and what not to do.

When it comes to loving her partner, a woman needs to love them in a way that is fulfilling for him as a man. Being aware of the presence of the man's alter ego is extremely important. He may not show his emotions, because in many respects it could be seen as a weakness and used against him.

In the privacy of the bedroom, however, a woman has to be compassionate and understanding that the male psyche requires validation and respect for the efforts he puts into providing a safe and secure haven for his family. It is her role to ensure that he feels safe and secure enough to go deep within himself to find that passion, to explore the emotional landscape of life, and fully connect spiritually.

When a man is deeply imbedded inside a woman, he is at his most vulnerable. Exposure of emotional vulnerability during love making requires deep trust. It is during these moments that men have the ability to stretch their love, deepen their soul and expose their vulnerabilities in the safety of their partner's arms.

An emotionally stable and secure female partner provides the man with an opportunity to open the door to emotional commitment. The power and strength of the woman's ability to embrace him and carry her partner through to the full tantric orgasm strengthens his emotional connection to his mate.

If a guy does not have this environment, then of course, men are quite happy to keep the emotional door closed and just have the physical release every couple of days, with whomever is willing to participate. This will probably keep most men physically satisfied enough to focus the rest of their time and efforts on work, hobbies, TV, or some other form of passing time.

If you truly want your man to feel loved, give him the freedom to do his work, respect his efforts for the family, provide a safe and confidential place to bear his soul, and willingly encourage the physical medium that allows him to connect emotionally and spiritually to himself, you, and the love for his family.

Pillow talk

One thing is clear: 'pillow talk' should be limited to the exploration of your partner, the passionate renewal of love conversations, the appreciation of the positives within your mate, and for the strengthening of the connections between your souls, journey, visions and dreams for your futures together.

If you are both angry, frustrated, or have too much on the mind, get up, make a cup of tea, and discuss what needs to be talked about in the lounge or dining room. Then come back to bed with a clear head and try to light the romantic fire again.

It is definitely clear that when females talk, they feel much better and lighter, and they can relax more once things are off their chest or mind.

Look into each other's eyes and hold each other's gaze. Look deeply, with care and acceptance, and lovingly at your partner. What are your feelings for them in that moment? What are some thoughts that arise in you about your partner?

They say the eyes are the windows to the soul, and yet how often do we actually look into each other's eyes. Maybe you used to do this a lot in the beginning of the relationship, but you have been together for a few years now and probably don't do it as regularly.

You have probably also been so caught up in the day-to-day intricacies of living and have forgotten to stop and actually look at each other without turning away to put the kettle on or do the dishes. Maybe you are searching the internet while your partner talks about their frustrations – are you really paying close attention to them then?

Yeah, yeah, I know, that's life!

In these moments, you can forget to be passionate. You can forget to engage fully into your relationship, and you can lose your intimacy because you have not made it your priority.

To fully commit to one another is the most beautiful, rewarding and important aspect of your relationship that will bring you through your life journey together. If you focus on ensuring you have a strong foundation for your relationship, you can be almost guaranteed to build a successful business together.

Male motivators and female motivators

We all understand that men and women are different. We are inbuilt with different motivators, priorities, and we comprise of totally different physical, mental and emotional attributes.

Somewhere in the dark recesses of your heart and mind, you know when something isn't quite right, or that what you are doing might be wrong – call it 'intuition', or maybe it is more a matter of how well we are connected with ourselves. I always say that if we ignore the signs, then at some point in time, *life* is going to hit us in the back of the head. We need to wake up. We need to take action when the little voice inside us alerts us that we are going down a dark pathway.

Men and male motivators

We can all take a good, long, hard look at the humorous side of the differences between men and women.

An Australian author, Mr Allan Pease, wrote a fabulous book: *Why Men Don't Listen and Women Can't Read Maps*. It is about a brilliant discovery into the differences between the sexes, and what goes on inside a male's and female's mind at various times[5]. It allows you to look at the funny side of your relationship interactions. However, there are also serious implications to the physical, mental and emotional make-up of men and women, and why we are built so differently.

It may sound very basic, but men have several modes – 'sex driven', 'work driven', 'hunter driven', 'food driven'. This means that for any given situation, they will either kill it, eat it, fix it or hump it. The male mind works differently to a woman's, as depicted in Mark Gungor's *Laugh Your Way To A Better Marriage* series – if men are not doing

---

5 Pease Allan, 2001. Penguin Random House Publishing, Australia

something productive, they are either sleeping or chilling in their 'nothing box'[6].

As women, we need to be aware of the differences and questions to ask such as:

> who is the man inside the man; how does he feel about himself and his role within the family and the business; and what comments from his partner supports or destroys the relationship?

I honestly believe that people who are dedicated to a purpose, particularly *men*, have a more positive view on life and themselves. Their self-worth increases as they step up into the 'protector/provider' role, also called the 'hunter/gatherer' role.

A man must feel like he is taking care of his partner and his family by providing for them on some level, and the greater the level, the better. Plus, he has to know, deep down, that his partner sees, understands and values this contribution. This places enormous pressure on the man. He will, by his very nature, carry this mantel silently, whether it is recognised or not.

---

6 Mark Gungor, Laugh Your Way To A Better Marriage – A Tale of Two Brains, viewed 30 August 2018, <https://www.youtube.com/watch?v=3XjUFYxSxDk>.

NOTE TO WOMEN

Please understand that if you undermine the man's purpose for 'protecting and providing' for his family, which includes you, it can be very destructive to the long-term survival of your relationship.

For men to function adequately and happily within a relationship, there are several things that they need along the way:
- Regular sex (his form of stress relief).
- Brain shut down time (thinking about absolutely NOTHING).
- Purposeful work.
- A hobby or Interest outside of work.
- Mates.
- A 'cave' /shed or den.
- An understanding, caring and supportive partner.

I have also seen situations where men are so focused on 'protecting and providing' for the family, that they work themselves so hard, day and night. It's not until a number of years later that they look up and the wife and family are gone. Oh, and she has taken the house, too. It is only then that the guy might wonder what went wrong. He was doing his best to protect and provide for the family, so why didn't the woman get that?

NOTE TO MEN

Remember, work is just work; however, the love of a good woman makes each day so much easier. Investing a little time with your partner is key to ongoing relationship happiness and success.

Sometimes it a case of: if only you can see ahead and take heed of the warnings that are all around you, you could change the way you do things, just a little, in order to make your future brighter and stronger.

So, women, here are some of the keys to understanding men.

Muscle power

For a man, his 'muscle' is everything he is – it's the way he dresses, how he speaks, the words that come out of his mouth, the way he walks, his actions, beliefs, core values, principles, and moral compass, also his masculinity, as well as the balance between masculine and feminine synergies within himself.

All these things combined create a presence around that man – the sort of thing that means that when he walks into a crowded room, everyone stops and stares at him. People are drawn to him naturally; he is kind and compassionate, patient with people's needs, and genuinely interested in who they are. These are generally the characteristics a man needs in order to attract his 'dream girl'.

Things that destroy the 'muscle' in a man could be getting drunk, or beating up a girl, cheating, making derogatory comments or jokes, or being too mucho or aggressive. All of these things will not attract a woman.

Male role models

Role models are people who have characteristics that you admire and wish to emulate. However, there are role models who abuse that trust, or who shatter their reputation by doing silly things, which is a shame. However, it is important for boys growing up to have a really good, strong male role model in their life. They need someone that they can look up to, respect and follow to guide them in becoming a great man.

Boys will learn from their male role models about how to treat the women in their lives. Like any child, they will either grow up to become exactly like their fathers, or completely different. We all follow the subtle learning from our upbringing a lot of the time, and we can choose to follow the same pathway or choose something that is the opposite.

For example, my current husband grew up in a household of violent binge drinkers and chain smokers. He could have either become a drinker and smoker himself, or not. As it so happened, he hated these vices and would never date someone who was like his foster parents. Instead, he plunged himself into cycling and competition sport, which was the complete opposite of how he was raised.

Don't forget that while you are on a journey of learning and growing, you are aspiring everyday to be better than you were the day before. At the same time, you are also very 'accepting' of yourself, just the way you are.

So, you may be asking, which statement is correct? Is the author confused or something? No, the answer is that both statements are correct.

There will be times when you need to accept that you are who you are and not expect too much of yourself, while at the same time, aspire to become a better person.

As with all things, the balance of the pendulum has to, and will, swing back. Hundreds of years ago, men used to rape and pillage enemy villages. Men ruled the earth and women were subservient, without a voice and without recognition. While this is not a woman's lib 'burning of the bra' book, it does ponder the question as to what the world will be like if the pendulum swung equal, and opposite, in an effort for Mother Earth to regain balance.

Maybe we can see some slight evidence of that happening already. Men sometimes are taken for everything they worked hard for when relationships fail. Kids from these failed relationships are usually then kept away from their fathers by 'court orders'. Women can fight aggressively for every inch of control or power over their ex-partners. And this can be a pain point for any man who has gone through a serious breakup. Whoever says that guys don't have emotions, well I would have to disagree with them. I think that is just not true, and I feel for any man who has had to suffer the wrath of an emotional and vengeful woman.

Women and female motivators

In case you were wondering, women are emotional creatures. It's like an explosion in our system that kicks in when we least expect it. Sometimes those emotions are out of control, and they need to be kept in check, otherwise a woman may suffer from 'Loopy Woman Syndrome'. This is a terrifying 'dis-ease' that creates a momentary lapse of sound reasoning and cripples even the strongest of women.

It usually happens when our emotions overrule any form of logic, reason or sensible conversation with another human being. Generally, if this is the case, we could say that the proverbial pendulum of the old grandfather clock has gone so far out of balance that it has come off its hinges all together.

As men are motivated by their sex drive, women are primarily steered by their emotional drive – the needs and desires of the heart. Without regular balancing, this can easily get out of hand. I have seen women send crazy text messages, write long and tearful letters, and even drive over to the new girlfriends place to slash their tyres or run keys down the side of their BMW. While I have never gone to the slashing tyres stage, I certainly have had my own share of emotional heartbreak.

So what are the priorities for women?

- To love and be loved exclusively.
- Nurture and care for the family unit.
- To be supported and be supportive.
- Protect the young and innocent.
- Enhance and strengthen the relationship.
- Ensure communication is open and flowing.
- Share problems and ease emotional burdens.
- Provide education and care for the children's growth and future.

For a woman, when there are stressful situations, or too much on the mind, the first thing that stops is sex. Our minds are constantly filled with emotional baggage that needs to come out. Sometimes women may allow the guy to have his way in the bedroom and then shove him off when it is all over. He is totally unaware that she is upset or frustrated because he has had his release. This lack of attention from the man in her life can build up inside a woman, with numbness and distain for the partner, who is not even considering her emotional needs.

Given time, it could turn into a lack of respect for him, as he lacks respect for her needs. It could even turn into resentment for the 'use' of her body to satisfy his own physical stress relief needs.

NOTE TO MEN

Women usually just need ten minutes of your time when you can give her 100% of your focus and really listen to her – this will go a long way toward opening the doorway to physical intimacy with her.

Women's priorities generally do not include sex. This is not a driving factor, or primal motivator for women. If we need to, we can live without it. Mind you, life will still be stressful for us.

Stress relief

Rest assured, there are great ways for women to relieve tension, such as massage, sunbathing, reading, and socialising. Once a woman has relaxed enough and cleared her mind of worry, she may be able to enjoy the wonderful sensations and climax that come with great sex. She will definitely want to spend more time with her partner in the bedroom.

Those women that have not experienced an orgasm will probably be the tetchy ones you meet at work or in social situations – uptight, slightly scary, and a little snappy with their comments. A happily relaxed woman will have more control over herself and be less likely to be clingy or needy on an emotional level. They will be more self-assured and definitely more comfortable with their own bodies.

Apart from being emotional, women crave a stable family unit. To have a wonderful partner that is faithful, caring, supportive, and a great provider and protector of the family unit is important to many woman. Her knight in shining armour will come and sweep her off her feet, take her away to his castle and they will live happily ever after. Oh, hang on, isn't that the 'fairytale' nonsense coming out again? But essentially, loyalty, strength, trust and respect are needed for women to thrive in any relationship. With that comes the trade-off for what guys want – sex.

NOTE TO WOMEN
Remember, sex is a physical male requirement, and using this as a manipulative tool to win emotional points will ultimately destroy your relationship.

Femme power

So if there is 'muscle' for men, what is there for women?

We have what is called our 'femme'. It is how we, as women, carry ourselves in society. It's the flower within us – our behaviour in public, our voice and tonality, posture, our walk, the grace through which we move about the room, our core values, principles and beliefs, and our 'moral compass'. The light that shines from within so to speak.

It's the complete opposite of the dreaded 'Loopy Woman Syndrome' – the crazy banshee that comes out when we are drunk, and who ends up lying in the gutter after a day at the races, with shoes off, mascara running, whiney high-pitched voice lamenting to her friends about anything and everything. If you have ever experienced a situation similar to this, well you just need to pick yourself up and get on with things.

You can become a new woman, fresh, proud and self-respectable enough to walk among society without being frowned upon. You have found yourself a great man, now you just need to hold on to him. Respect him and cherish his needs. Treat him like a king, and set your simple yet clear non-negotiables to guide him to treating you like his queen.

It might sound all a little fluffy and fairytale-like, but what if I was to tell you that this is your opportunity to create your own fairytale, right here, with the man (or woman) who is sitting beside you. That is the person you have made a commitment to and chosen to take the journey of life together with. You are here now, reading this book because you want to make both of your lives better. To build a stronger relationship with the person you love, and with that, build a stronger business together as well.

Things that destroy the 'femme' – well, obviously the girl in the gutter is a classic, albeit very public, display of lost 'femme'. However, there are more subtle ways that women can destroy their 'femme' and thereby make themselves 'less attractive' to the opposite sex.

Here are a few examples:
- Constant nagging.
- Public humiliation of your partner.
- Name-calling.
- Spitefulness or aggressive behaviour.
- Yelling and screaming / screeching.
- Superficial or being money hungry.
- Gossiping.
- Irrational emotional outbursts (not including standard venting of general daily frustrations).
- Over-sexualised public behaviour.
- Indecent speech or behaviours.
- Being dismissive of your partner and their efforts.

For females, our best options are to disarm as many of the emotionally reactive 'triggers' as possible. Because we come with a load of them, it shouldn't be too hard to find a few to sort out. Once our partner sees some changes within us, this will help them to draw closer to us. If you have exhibited any of the above behaviours in the past, and your partner has been hiding in the 'dog house', it might feel safer for him to step back inside the house once you disarm your triggers.

Creating a safe and less-explosive household will go a long way to easing tension between the two of you. You need to calm the waters, reignite the warm hearth, settle into the couch with a doona, a bottle of wine, and start to chat together about why you both came into the relationship and what your hopes and dreams were in the first place.

Talk about the things that attracted you to each other in the beginning. What is the ultimate dream lifestyle you both want to achieve? Share your thoughts and visions together one evening when it is just to two of you.

The purpose is to recognise each other's great points and support each other's goals. Often we don't know what we cannot see in ourselves, so be gentle, loving and supportive of your partner's feelings as they transition through to being more aware of themselves.

Infidelity

Years ago while holidaying, my husband and I sat in a restaurant near a young couple and the guy's mate dining together. The atmosphere around their table seemed a little awkward. As I studied their behaviour, it became quite evident that the girlfriend was trying desperately to draw her boyfriend into a conversation, and yet he was quite clearly wishing he were somewhere else – with someone else.

The boyfriend's mate appeared to hang his head in embarrassment, as if he knew of the illicit affair going on, to which the girl was blissfully unaware. However, to maintain some form of pretend harmony, the two guys kept quiet, while the girlfriend bubbled away with oblivious chatter towards them.

I could tell that the boyfriend had been in this situation for more than a couple of months, and that this guy was no longer in love with his girlfriend. However, to maintain some sort of temporary harmony, he formed a pattern of behaviour that allowed him to manage the situation without it getting out of control – in a screaming fit of 'Loopy Woman Syndrome' – in front of all the surrounding holidaying guests enjoying their meals.

Now, if you were in our situation, would you hope that the boyfriend would eventually tell her of his affair, or that she found out some other way, or is she better off being blissfully ignorant to the whole situation until she is ready to come to terms with it?

The point is that hindsight gives us 20/20 vision – most of the time. Some people, even after the 'experience' of their partner having an affair, still can't see how or why it happened.

So what if we could see the signs more readily? As I mentioned earlier, there are always warning signs or 'guideposts' that will point towards a certain 'experience' – good, bad or indifferent. We generally just need to go through these experiences to become better people, or to form new patterns of behaviour.

Respect

'Truth' and 'respect' are my two non-negotiables, as 'trust' is built upon truth and respect. They are big-ticket items on the 'core values' chart in many people's viewpoint. It is not until you are without either one of these things that it really starts to matter, and yet we probably don't do enough to protect these things when we *do* have them.

I will discuss 'truth' below; however, let's look at 'respect' first.

Respect is not something that just disappears one day. Respect disintegrates very slowly and subtly at first – be it a flippant comment or an unaccomplished request.

It silently erodes away at a relationship, sometimes for many years before any realisation hits you. You look across the table at the person you have been living with, or at the least co-habiting with, and realise that the respect for them is long gone, and you cannot remember when you last truly loved them unconditionally. A sense of sadness seeps in as you recognise that a lack of respect can dull your romance, your spark, and the chemistry that made life exciting and mysterious in the beginning.

My youngest daughter, Michelle, was a talented artist in primary school. When most kids were drawing stick figures, she had a beautiful eye for detail and added depth and soul to her artwork. I was so impressed by her skills that I went and purchased a load of art stuff – paints, paper, canvas and charcoal. Happy to encourage her work, I knew that art helped her relax, and she enjoyed it.

I am pretty sure that Michelle was happiest when she was drawing – it was like an escape for her. All was going well until one day, my ex-husband opened his mouth with some ridiculously flippant comment like, 'You need to find another career, Michelle, 'cos the only good artist is a dead one'. Sadly, Michelle never drew again after that.

As you can imagine, I lost a lot of respect for him that day.

Maybe it was just said in ignorance, not realising the consequences of his statements, nor understanding the impact that it would have on someone else. Maybe it was said to intentionally hurt me through her. People do that sometimes – they will use whatever method or possible angle to spark a reaction when they themselves are in pain.

Resentment

Many people find in the early stages of the relationship that they only have eyes for each other. The trick is to *keep* that going – long after the honeymoon phase is over. As time ticks by, decisions made against our better judgement, mistakes, or failings of business decisions or relationship efforts may also cause a loss of respect, and eventually resentment breeds within the relationship. So how do we stop the downward spiral of negativity that leads to resentment of our partner?

All problems stem from the source. Violence stems from anger, and anger from pain. So too, resentment stems from harbouring negative thoughts. Anywhere there is an imbalance, people will challenge the status quo. There will be an inequality evident within the relationship, which could be subtle in attitude or obvious in work capacity.

The same thing happens when you see, acknowledge, or have a solid negative thought about a fault or failure within your partner. Looking in from the outside, it is so easy to pass comment or judge another person for what they say or do, how they act or not act, which in your opinion is an undesirable trait. Your view of them is then tarnished in some way. The more you see this, the worse it becomes, until you are frustrated and start to push back onto them a form of judgement or disdain. This is the beginning of 'resentment'.

When resentment is then expressed, it can become the wedge that drives between a couple's relationship. It will test the very limits of their commitment to each other and the business. If you feel there may be some imbalance happening, speak up early, discuss a solution and fix the problem before it gets way out of hand.

Building respect

So how would we build respect for each other?

It's really very simple – ignore the bad and focus on the good things.

Every morning and every evening, I tell my husband that he is the king of my world – my perfect husband. I thank him every day for being so wonderful, and I express appreciation for every effort he makes towards our common goals. I focus on his great qualities that make him so endearing: his softness, his gentleness, and his light-heartedness. Without him I would be too serious.

Sure, I could easily focus on the downsides of his personality. He is lazy, frustratingly slow, non-assertive, wishy-washy and indecisive.

Of course I could see the negatives, in fact that would be the easiest thing in the world for me to do, because I am a 'Driver' who has terrible downsides, such as bullying, being unemotional, intolerant, aggressive, judgemental, too fast, stubborn and cold.

In fact, combine that with the 'Analytical' side of my nature and I can be particularly fussy, critical and revengeful. But I know that is not the type of person I want to be for myself. I love myself enough to know that. I don't want to live my life without friends, without love, companionship or support. So, I don't allow those parts of my personality profile to take hold. I deliberately make sure that I don't focus on the negatives.

Instead, I take time to write messages to my husband, thanking him for all his wonderful support. Thanking and appreciating his qualities every day helps in two ways. Firstly, it reminds me to always see the positives. Secondly, it boosts his desire to continue helping, supporting and working well alongside me.

Trust

When couples are in a relationship, everything hinges on their ability to trust each other.

'Truth' begets 'trust'.

Being truthful with each other, about ourselves and how we feel, goes a long way to building that trust *together*. We have to build trust in the relationship, both with love and emotions, as well as with our combined financial situation. Being in business together leverages even greater financial risk, against both partner's home and their business assets. It is no good if one person does all the hard work while the other is off spending all the money.

Having both incomes coming from the same business is extremely tough, because if something happens with that business, there is no fallback, no safety net. Some couples opt for having one person take extra shifts or work elsewhere, and they may take on a 'part-time' role within the business, just to ensure there is a stable income for the bills.

Whatever your situation, you are both in this together, and you are both therefore reliant on 'trust' and 'respect' for each other and your common goals to make your relationship and business successful.

Trust in business

Many business couples who have separated in their personal lives but who continue working the business successfully together have admitted that the key reason the business relationship survives is because they trust each other implicitly with each other's ability to run the business well and to protect the financial interests together.

Acceptance of our own humanness is a gracious and humbling virtue. It is a gift that is at the very core of any successful relationship. No one wants to be judged, disrespected or undervalued, especially by our partner, so having strong clarity about our own self-worth and the value of the contributions that our partner brings is significantly important into building a strong and enjoyable future together.

See the great things in others, lift up their good qualities before their eyes, and focus your personal thoughts on seeing the best in other people. If you do all of this and the person does not respond positively by demonstrating their good qualities more often, then maybe they don't actually want these positives to be who they truly are. They may prefer being obnoxious, aggressive, or vindictive, in which case, politely say, 'Thank you for being who you are' and walk away.

You are entitled to surround yourself with positive and uplifting people, but also remember to be one of those people yourself. Always 'thank' the other person for who they are – good, bad or indifferent – as they have shown you their true colours. If those colours are not bringing out the best in *you*, then that person has obviously shown you that it is time to leave before they destroy you altogether. Knowing that gives you the strength to walk away, and *that* is a very good day.

Why couples argue

Seeing as you and your partner are humans, sometimes it doesn't matter the degree of your commitment, or how well you attain a balance with all aspects discussed above, as you will have disagreements and argue. It is bound to happen.

So how can you rise above these instances for the sake of your relationship, both personally and professionally? Let's discuss this more closely.

A life without any form of stress can be a bad thing.

Imagine if there was never anything even slightly related to pressure or stress in your life. What would that look like? For many of you reading this book, it might sound like your dream holiday right now, am I right?

There always has to be a balance, for sure, but what if there was *never* any stress? What if no one ever got angry, or pushed for something to happen? Or what if no one was ever in a hurry, or needed to go somewhere that was important? We would ultimately lose our sense of urgency about things.

There would be nothing to actually motivate us to achieve anything in our lives. No need to get out of bed or rush to complete a task for any form of deadline. Whatever half-finished project would be considered acceptable, as no one would bother about complaining.

A little bit of constructive anger is a good thing. It forces us to change things in our lives that we are dissatisfied with. It helps us to find a better way of doing things that are tiresome or labour intensive. Note the key is 'constructive anger', not the destructive type, which means a person just goes on a rampage, destroying things and breaking stuff to make a point.

If someone is whining about their circumstances, but they are not doing anything about it, then it is usually because they are not frustrated or angry enough to move, shift or change their situation. They are probably quite happy to 'vent' their problems, but they are not willing to get off their bum and change their circumstances. Getting a new job, or throwing out that old desk – anything that needs to be done, but hasn't yet been done, is generally never done because the issue hasn't grinded the person enough that they get up off their couch and do something to change that issue.

Anger, fear, and many other strong emotions can create stress and pressure for anyone, especially for couples in business. Because you are so intricately linked to one another, the stress is often magnified across both parties if you don't manage it properly.

However, the benefits of having two of you in a relationship, as well as sharing the load in business, means that one person can have a break if they are feeling overly stressed etc. while the other one can continue to hold the fort temporarily.

Taking time out from the situation will allow each person to have the opportunity to cope better. Even if it's just for half an hour, whatever is needed to allow the more stressed of the two to walk outside, collect their thoughts and realign their balance, or in some cases, disarm a 'trigger' if things are significantly stressful.

Constructive conflict

We all see things from different viewpoints, as explained in the beginning of this book. This is particularly true when working with your partner in your business together. You will naturally have different ways of achieving a task, and when someone does it differently to you, it may cause conflict. Everyone is trying to push ahead in their own way, and some people give in more easily, while others find it difficult to let go.

Conflict is there to assist with increasing the opportunity to learn. Sometimes we are not always aware of the lesson that we need to learn, or the information we need to understand, during the heat of the moment.

Constructive conflict stretches your current thinking and skills, and it pushes you to reach out more into the unknown, outside of what you currently know. Constructive conflict focuses on situations, things, events and facts. Destructive conflict focuses on attacking people, feelings, values and beliefs.

It is imperative not to resort to name-calling, yelling or aggressiveness during any form of conflict. Removing the emotional attachments and discussing facts and relevant information, and then working together to find a solution is more important than proving yourself to be 'right'.

Make a choice to not argue about things, but have constructive discussions with solution-based outcomes, and negotiate the best for both of you to create an easier life, with less stress and greater romance together. Communicating well is the key to more constructive solutions for the challenges you will face in business and in love.

Disarming emotional 'triggers'

Conflict will inevitably bring about strong emotions. So, you must learn how to disarm the emotional explosions or 'triggers' that happen within yourself whenever you enter into some form of conflict. This sounds simple enough; however, it is not always easy because the challenge comes when looking within yourself to find the cause behind your overwhelming emotion.

Everyone carries around emotional baggage. Some people handle this better than others, often by pushing thoughts to one side and ignoring the obvious issues that need to be dealt with. It could be a family or work issue. Whatever the reason, often sorting through the problem seems more difficult than it is worth in effort. So we lock that subject in a box, and as long as nothing is mentioned, it will stay safely hidden, for the rest of our lives. A sign on the top of the box says: 'Do Not Open', and like poking a sleeping bear, if it does 'open' there is no guarantee for anyone's safety.

I've given this quite a bit of thought, and let me explain like this . . .

Every human being on the face of this earth is *physiologically* the same. When I am happy, I laugh. When you are happy, you laugh. When I am sad, I cry, and when you are sad, you cry. Physiologically our body's reactions to emotions will manifest in similar ways.

Anger will manifest itself in the same way in each and every human being – tightness in the body muscles, a lump in the throat, an increase in blood pressure, stiffening of the torso and upper body.

So, if we are *all* the same physiologically, what makes us *different*?

I believe that it's the 'triggers' that make us different. Our life experiences, our beliefs, our values, our personality traits, the way we process our thinking, defence mechanisms, behaviours and life perspectives make us different from each other.

What makes one person happy may make someone else confused. What makes one person extremely sad may have absolutely no effect on someone else.

For us to not only understand that we are all different, but to also learn to respect each other's differences is one of the biggest relationship challenges in life.

Disarming your 'triggers' means actually letting go, once and for all, of a piece of 'baggage' that holds you back from being the best version of yourself. Most of your 'baggage' can be identified by your attitude towards things or situations.

If one person has a particularly strong viewpoint, something that they refuse to let go of, even though there is evidence to the contrary, it is most likely due to an underlying emotional 'trigger', or because of the pain that causes the reason behind the stronghold over their firmly held position. There may be a past experience or belief that has cemented a defence mechanism in place, in order to protect them emotionally from dealing with some form of painful realisation.

Emotional 'triggers' are feelings that have a strong connotation for you as a person. For example, they may be feelings of anger, jealousy, fear, guilt, sadness or frustration. All strong emotions have a reason behind them, and because every person is different based upon these 'triggers', each person will have different reasoning for the emotional response.

I read a book once by Gary Zukav, titled *The Heart of the Soul*, and he talks about 'emotions' being like the guiding curbs of the road that we travel along in life. The book explained for me a lot about life, and my understanding was that when we hit a strong emotion, it was like we started to go off the pathway, and we had to essentially 'hit the kerb', as Gary Zukav explains[7]. For me, this indicates a 'trigger' that is stopping us from becoming the best version of ourselves as we travel down the road of life.

I like to think of it like this: imagine a diamond buried at the bottom of a pile of dirty rocks. Some rocks are big and others are smaller. However, one fact remains, you cannot stand on the very top of the pile of rocks and put your hand straight down through the centre to the bottom and pick up the diamond.

One has to remove the top rocks and then some more, until the pile becomes smaller. Then once most of the rocks have been removed, only then can you start to see the diamond at the bottom of the pile.

Like the rocks, each of us has many emotional triggers that we discover about ourselves. Start by disarming the smaller ones on the top of the pile, then as you let go, you will come closer to the diamond within you – the centrepiece of your true and ultimate value and potential.

There is a process that can take you on the journey of discovery about where the 'trigger' begins, which is important, as without understanding where the source of the emotion originates, it is very difficult to disarm the power that the emotion will have over you in life. It's kind of like pulling a thread on a knitted jumper – the unravelling

---

7   Zukav, G 2002,*The Heart of the Soul*, Simon & Schuster Ltd, London, United Kingdom.

of the emotional timeline will eventually come back to the source of the pain point.

Again the best way to describe this is with a story:

Let's imagine an old lady sitting in a bingo hall with her friends. She has her game in front of her, and one of her friends distracts her from the announcement of the next number, which is the number she had. As she turns away, someone else calls out 'BINGO' and wins the game. The old lady's emotional response may be one of upset and anger, because someone else won the game that she should have won.

The emotional 'trigger' is therefore activated and the old lady laments about how it is unfair, and that she 'always misses out on things'. 'Always' is one of those endless words.

Pulling on the thread of that endless word, we can discover that the old lady has regularly 'missed out' during the course of her life. She may be able to give several examples; however, the part that hurts the most is when she was four years old. Sitting under the Christmas tree was a present that she desperately wanted, and yet it was for someone else. The pain and rejection she felt as a child has caused her to emotionally respond to a culmination of every single incident that she 'missed out on' throughout her life.

So, the pattern is formed previously, but the 'trigger' manifests itself as an emotional reaction to something inconsequential, as the cycle repeats itself over and over again. If we disarmed that 'trigger' by addressing the four year olds 'pain points', then the old lady in the bingo hall would more likely have laughed off the fact that she was distracted by her friend and missed her cue for the winning number.

Follow your strong emotions and ask yourself: 'Why do I feel like this?'; 'Where did I first get this feeling?; 'Why do I have this feeling?'; 'What caused it?'

Once you have discovered how and where you first felt a certain way, it is almost like an epiphany, as you feel the 'ah ha moment' when it all seems to make sense.

When you get the 'ah ha moment', you know that you have just disarmed that 'trigger'. From then on, that particular issue should not bother you anymore. Keep in mind, however, that there are often several aspects to the situation that will have several different threads and triggers for you. So keep following the process and you will help relieve a great deal of stress and 'baggage' from your life.

Sometimes, I need help with my partner when I ask myself the 'Why' questions, and his help can assist me in focusing on following the thread to the source of my emotional pain points. If your partner is assisting you with this process, then they will also learn more about you, and it can help to open the lines of communication between you both and build stronger relationship bonds together.

Remember to be gentle on yourself and others through this process, as it can be quite challenging to open up and share your deepest emotions. However, the best thing is that you are safest with your partner by your side during this exercise. Share this process with love for each other, and you will succeed in creating renewed passion, acknowledging strengths and weaknesses of your humanity, and accepting each other for who you are. This is called 'unconditional love'.

SECTION FOUR

You get in life what you have
the courage to ask for.

Oprah Winfrey

COMMUNICATION

Our most intricate tool for building relationships and strengthening our ability to work well with another person resides in our ability to communicate effectively. What you say, and often what you don't say, can communicate enough information to either help you to flourish or ultimately destroy whatever you have with your partner.

Communication is not just about talking *at* someone, but also listening, interpreting, understanding, and responding appropriately. Research shows that only 7% of all communication is actually the words that are spoken, while 93% of communication comes down to body language and vocal intonations[8].

In this section you will discover the nuances behind communicating effectively together, and how to open the channels between you both in order to ensure you are heading in the same direction. If two people

---

8   Fields J 2018, *Speaking Without Words: Body Language and Non-Verbal Cues in* Communication, Lifesize, viewed 10 March 2018, <https://www.lifesize.com/en/video-conferencing-blog/speaking-without-words>.

are trying to achieve something great, then working together towards the end goal needs to be discussed and agreed upon. You need to both be on the same page.

If both people in the relationship are pulling in different directions, then the forces will cancel each other out and nothing will be achieved. You will be putting in great effort for very little return on investment of your time and energy. This becomes counter-productive and frustrating, and it is the beginning of a very destructive process.

With renewed commitment between the two of you, by now you should be at least in a position where you are starting to understand that you need to enhance your ability to communicate effectively.

So what does that look like? How do we communicate properly and effectively to ensure that we are being heard by the other person? How do we speak up and tell them how we feel? Much of it comes down to preparation and timing.

This is about identifying and harnessing the individual skillsets that each partner brings to the table, and then establishing value, respect, trust and integrity to the communication between two people. There are great highs and lows in the business journey, to which each person within the partnership needs to support the other as they weather the storm together. A couple's intimacy is usually always increased when renewed communication strategies and tools are discovered.

What is effective communication?

Communication is as much about listening as it is about understanding the message and thinking carefully about the appropriate response. Life would be easier if all communication was fashioned this way; however, in a relationship and working together, the emotionally intertwined love/hate banter that normally slides between work time and home time can lose the discernable clear line that is needed to stop the two from mixing.

Effective communication is saying what you mean and meaning what you say. Easier said than done, I know, because you often get caught up in the moment of the conversation, and you can't think of the right words to explain exactly how you feel about something at the time. Maybe you are in the middle of a discussion and the major points to your argument have flown out the window. You can sometimes walk away from an argument and about a day later start thinking of all the clever statements you should have said yesterday.

There are studies that show that when you are under pressure, your mind can temporarily stop processing information, which is why without planned speeches, some presenters have not had the flow of communication that is needed at the most critical moment of their presentation.

The flow of information that travels between two people has to be clear and concise. During any communication, it is the 'speaker's' responsibility to clearly convey their message. It is the person speaking who has to make sure that the person listening has understood them correctly.

For the 'listener', it is their responsibility to pay attention and to clarify the information back to the speaker to ensure that they have received the information correctly.

I like to think of it like this: if I wanted to travel to a friend's place that I had never been to before, and she told me to go past the roundabout, take the second left and the first right, and then come to a house with a green letterbox, and after that I had to take the second right, and then go past the yellow house on the corner with the blue-heeler dog . . .

Can you see the problem here?

Yep . . . you lost me at 'roundabout'.

Give me the actual address and I can find it using 'Google Maps'.

Sending our communication to another person has to be clearly articulated. The person must be able to hear and understand you.

If you are the 'listener', there may be times when you cannot identify the main point the person communicating is trying to convey. You may need to pull them up and say, 'May I ask a question?'

While you may know what information you are seeking, your partner may not. Listening and understanding the question is key to effective communication. Answering with the relevant information completely and concisely is critical to ensure the message is presented clearly. The 'speaker' may give a bunch of other irrelevant information; however, they might not actually answer your original question.

You may need to tell the 'speaker' that the actual question has not been answered and give them a chance to acknowledge that what they have said isn't clear and understandable, so they are then given a chance to express themselves again.

Be authentic and consistent with your verbal and non-verbal communication. You need to make sure that you are communicating effectively, with a purpose to achieve stronger relationships or work better together in building and growing your business. Be clear and concise about your needs and requests, and if needed you can note down the required actions and responsibilities or agreed tasks.

There are plenty of courses and books on effective communication that will help if you are finding difficulty in the smoothness of conversation and understanding between you and your partner. Take into account the different personality types and understand that some personality styles are okay with sitting together in silence, while other personality types are very uncomfortable with silence. Understanding each other's personality will also help in identifying the best ways to communicate together, especially when under extreme pressure.

Signs of communication disaster

You know when communication is falling apart – when you switch off during conversations, or maybe you are disagreeing silently but are afraid to speak your mind or open the discussion. Effective communication involves listening, processing and understanding, as well as reciprocation of ideas and conversation.

Obviously there are keys to effective communication, such as not speaking over one another, and respecting one another's point of view. Tonality, eye contact, voice modulation and all other specific techniques can assist in ensuring that you do not misunderstand what your partner is attempting to say.

Emotional arguments

Take time out for communicating the important things that need to be said or discussed. Say exactly what you are intending to say; however, don't make bold statements and throw words around, especially during an argument. Be careful using endless words such as 'always', 'never', 'forever' and 'everyone'.

We often say things in the heat of the moment, and then we wish we hadn't said them. We say things to shock the other person, or take control of the direction of the conversation. In the middle of an argument, many things can be said that either intentionally or unintentionally hurt the other person.

'You don't really mean that, do you?'

'Yes, I do mean it.'

And you very well might think you mean what you said at the time, and yet a few hours later, when your emotions have calmed down, you may feel a sense of regret and realise that you probably didn't quite mean it in that particular way. There may be things that need to be said afterwards to clarify your intent, or you may need to apologise for saying something you really don't want to have out there.

Venting

'Venting' is a pressure-relief valve that we all have. It takes the top layer of frustrations from us temporarily and relieves a little of that emotional build-up that we carry around from time to time. People 'vent' or 'let off steam' in different ways – for some it is heavy exercise, and for others it can be by crying or laughing, but mostly it can be by yelling or arguing.

Once you have 'vented' your emotions, you probably feel much better. Even if the problem is not solved, you have the emotional relief inside that allows you to pick up and carry on for another day.

For couples in business together, recognise 'venting' for what it is, just that, a simple explosion of emotional outburst that is a temporary relief for the other person.

Listening without judgement

You do not need to take 'venting' personally, or even try to fix anything for the person who is 'venting', just let the steam come out and then the lid will close and all will be calm again. Once the dust settles, then a logical and reasonable discussion can be had about how to solve whatever issue is still challenging the relationship. Remember to 'vent' your frustrations at situations, not at other people. Especially those you love.

For any successful relationship to prosper during communication, it is imperative to remove blame, accusations, negativity and judgements from your communication. Emotionally charged arguments can be self-destructive, and they can also disintegrate the relationship. If you are feeling emotional, then you may need to remove yourself, take a breather, and disarm some triggers before attending to the conversation again when everyone is more relaxed and calm.

Classic motion

We tend to fall into patterns of communication that I call 'classic motion'. These are when we give standard responses that avoid open-ended discussions between two adults in a frank and liberating manner. Often these patterns are found as you go through the supermarket checkout and the cashier asks you, 'How are you today?' Your automatic response is usually, ' Yeah, good thanks.' You know they don't really care how you are, they are just paid to say that to every customer.

You may be having the worst day ever, but it's not the cashier's responsibility to be a good 'listener' for you right then and there. So you respond with something that allows you to keep the conversation to a minimum so you can get the hell out of there quickly.

In reality, we want to minimise this 'classic motion' response in conversations with our partner.

'What's wrong?' is another question that you probably come across frequently with your partner. The answer of 'nothing' is a 'classic motion' response. While there may in fact be nothing wrong, because it is a standardised pattern of responsive communication, our partners tend to not believe you, and so they dig a little deeper, saying, 'Come on, something must be wrong', and the cycle quickly becomes frustrating for both partners.

To break the habits of 'classic motion', you have to be aware of your automatic responses in any given situation and change the words so that you can provide a reasonable and logical explanation that does not carry any emotional backlash in the background.

Instead, you can say something like, 'I'm fine, just thinking about yesterday's conversation with Mike, about the car'; or, 'I'm actually not thinking anything, I'm just enjoying the scenery'. This way, your partner understands that you have things on your mind, or you are just chilling and enjoying the peace and quiet.

Effective communication between people is not about justifying yourself all the time, but providing enough detail in the conversation in order to help the other person understand how you are feeling.

We all make mistakes

Part of being together in a relationship with someone is that they know your 'downsides', and yes, we all have them! Someone else sees your mistakes, and so you can't really hide this. You have to be authentic with your partner because they are your support in life and in business.

There will be mistakes that both of you make in business, decisions that cost the business, and sometimes the price you pay is high, other times, not so much. Rest assured, everyone in business makes mistakes. Because you are together, you also have the awful task of owning up to the mistake to our partner. And that can be tough because you just *know* the conversation that follows next.

'How the F*^~did that happen?'

There will most likely be a few hours of ranting and raving by your partner, until they eventually calm down and come to terms with the magnitude of the problem, and then together you can set about working out how you can fix the mess.

The point is, the last thing you want to do in this process is magnify the mistakes that your partner has made, or make them feel guilty for being human. You have to bring out your accepting side, which can be really difficult to do. Obviously the pain of the mistake or whatever the consequences are can be extremely tough to forgive and forget sometimes.

While it is easy for me to say, 'just get over it', the reality is not that simple.

Once again, our strategy here is to focus on the positive processes rather than highlighting and giving more energy to feed the negative communication cycle that surrounds our thoughts, actions and conversation.

Realising and accepting that a mistake has happened can be 80% of the battle, because you know that you are both human, so it is no surprise that mistakes will happen.

The best strategy is to take a 'proactive' approach and own up as soon as possible, saying, 'I'm so sorry, but I stuffed up'. This a line that always works because you admit to the fault as soon as you find it, and you apologise and acknowledge that you made a mistake.

What makes things worse is when you try to hide it, cover it up, or blame someone else. These things only serve to bring you back to the 'trust' and 'respect' issue we spoke about earlier. Without honesty, especially when it matters most, then the respect dies and all you have proven to your partner is that you are trying to deliberately hide the truth from them.

There may be situations where you genuinely do not know that something bad has happened until after your partner finds out. In any case, honesty is the best answer. Once two people can feel safe and comfortable in owning up to mistakes with their partner, the sooner the both of you can begin working on solutions.

One person speaking at a time

Within any relationship, you have to offer something of value to the other person. Generally, these things that you offer are explored during the courting phase of any relationship. In business, however, you may choose different skills that are on offer by a person during the recruitment phase and interviewing process. And when you are life partners and suddenly working together in a business, you have to be really skilled in many different areas, as well as being able to adjust between work mode and home mode.

My husband and I are great life partners; however, it was not until several years into our relationship that we decided to explore working in a business together. We both recognised and valued each other's skill set, so we felt confident that we could achieve success together. William is great at fixing things, while I am good at business administration.

Together we built a business servicing office equipment for other small businesses. We fit a nice niche market where our services are specialised yet affordable for most businesses that need office equipment, such as a reliable printer, but they don't want to be caught in an expensive contract to a large corporation for the use of that equipment.

We are fortunate to have fallen into a brilliant business model that is both profitable and in demand, with plenty of ongoing work, so we don't really need to do much marketing or hunt for customers. Most of our business has grown through word of mouth.

We started four and a half years ago (at the time of writing this book) with two customers, and we worked from our garage. We now have over 700 customers and are continuing to grow. We are currently designing a revolutionary franchise model where the franchisee reaps more of the profits than the franchisor. I call it 'revolutionary', because for many couples in business together, franchising has taken a huge toll on them emotionally and financially.

In fact, I have seen firsthand the devastation of those that have failed, including my ex-husband and myself when we worked together in the coffee shop franchise we owned. It was soul-destroying, working 80 plus hours a week for less than 50 cents an hour. The hardships caused by franchise giants that totally destroy the franchisee's livelihoods, sending their entire lifetime of savings down the tube so that the franchiser can sit back and collect high franchise fees, is not where William and I believe small business should be.

To make sure our business is successful together, William and I are usually ticking along, yet we often openly validate each other's contributions. William admits freely that if he did this business on his own, it would never have gone this far. He is great at the technical side, but terrible when it comes to issuing a bill for his services.

By the same token, I validate openly and recognise that without my husband, I would definitely struggle to do this business on my own. I need someone like him to build customer relationships, create opportunities, and also fix things that are broken. We work well together as a team.

I have seen businesses whereby one partner does 80% and the other person does 20%. Sometimes the workload is shared 50/50. Maybe, one person looks after the home and family while the other runs the business single-handed. The point to the 20% or the 50%, whatever the balance or equality of tasks are, is that each person has to validate whatever contribution their partner is making.

Appreciation and validation

Appreciation goes a long way. Without validation, there is no appreciation of your partner's support in the business and life. Appreciation essentially makes your efforts enjoyable. If your work and life are both enjoyable, then you will be more inclined to do more and give more of yourself in the relationship and in building the business.

It's not rocket science; however, I think that we can get caught up in the daily grind of living and business. We allow things to overwhelm us, and with all the pent-up emotional, mental and physical stress, we forget to take a few moments to stop and appreciate how well we have done as individuals and as a partnership.

Remember to stop the negative thoughts and judgements, because doing that is the easy way out. Focus on the *positive contributions* that your partner has made this week to the success of your joint business. Focus on all the great skills that they bring to your relationship and business together.

Write down a list of aspects you appreciate in your partner, and then have each person speak (one at a time) about all these positive appreciations that you have identified. Work on ways you can both bring your 'A-game' to work and at home to build a successful life. Validate, recognise, respect and communicate all the positives, and pretty soon it will be easier to see why you are able to build such a great future together.

Agree to disagree– talking about the tough stuff

You have probably established by now that men aren't really into sharing their feelings so much, unlike women. However, sometimes men won't see that there are important things that do need discussing occasionally. And sometimes these things that pertain to the relationship or the business can ruffle some feathers in the nest.

Not many people will put their hands up and admit that they love 'conflict'. I can't say that 'no one' wants that, because I have met a couple of people who *do* love conflict. They thrive on it. You might have met some people like that, and maybe you avoid them like the plague because they will deliberately create arguments and stress where there is none. They will somehow manufacture conflict from thin air, and suddenly you find yourself in the middle of it all, with nowhere to run.

Whenever there are important things on my mind, and I am talking about significant discussions or decisions that need to be made, I find that the best thing is for me to disarm the emotional 'trigger' that is behind it for me. That way, when I do approach my partner, it is without the full force of an emotional outburst behind it.

Emotions can drive harsh words through the heart of any situation, like a tsunami. There is no stopping any discussion that flows on the top of that wave of destruction. The words are out and sweeping devastation through the relationship, and before you know it, the relationship is in shreds, and the rebuilding can take years, if ever.

Challenging conversations

So how do you approach topics that are really challenging and difficult?

The answer is to do it very carefully.

Be respectful of each other's point of view, and remember that everyone has their own corner of the intersection, and each person has the right to express their truth. Everyone deserves respect and acceptance for who they are as people.

In such situations, I always pre-empt the conversation with, 'Honey, I just need to let you know how *I feel* right now'.

Please be aware that using emotional blackmail during any conversation about tough stuff can be extremely counter-productive. Laying blame or using guilt, as a methodology to turn the conversation around in order to gain the upper ground, will only destroy the other person's perception of you, and you then lose their respect.

Remember that with all these tools, *no* person can *make* you do something that you don't want to do. If you find yourself in an emotionally blackmailing situation, and you are falling back into the pattern of behaviour where the other person is gaining hold over you, or has power over you, then you need to stop and reassess your position.

Controlling and manipulating conversations

People who are at the mercy of someone else are usually there because they have allowed the other person to fulfil a deep and dark 'urgent need' somewhere inside. Maybe they 'need to be needed', or they are 'too scared to be alone'. Whatever this deep and dark motivator is, that person becomes trapped within a destructive relationship that they can't seem to escape.

There is a book called *Tricky People* written by Andrew Fuller, and this book covers many of the different tactics that people use to manipulate communication and objectives in order to gain the upper hand[9]. If you have a feeling that things are not quite right within your relationship, but you can't seem to place your finger on exactly what the problems are, this is a great book to uncover the hidden agendas of different people around you. This can be applicable for all manner of relationships – friendships, work colleagues or acquaintances.

The only way to stop the merry-go-round of life is to bring everything to the conscious awareness. By openly saying to the person, 'Are you trying to emotionally blackmail me?' will force the transparency of their motive.

No one can hide a secret if the secret is already spoken out loud to the room. No one can hide an item, if that item is already on the table

---

[9] Fuller, A 2013,*Tricky People: How to deal with horrible types before they ruin your life*, Harper Collins Publishers Pty Ltd, Australia.

in front of everyone. To disarm any form of manipulation, you have to call it out loud. Speak up and identify the action or behaviour.

Having difficult conversations can take a bit of preparation. While not everyone is as blunt and straight up as myself, it can take a lot of courage to speak up at the right time, or in the middle of an argument. While we don't want the aggression to be turned towards us, it does help diffuse situations when trying to find out what the purpose is behind someone's action, or their 'in-action'.

To disarm and disorientate anyone who is being tricky or who is manipulating a situation, ask a question from left field. Ask them something such as, 'Why do you do that?' When the person responds with, 'Do what?', you can explain the problem and the consequence of their actions or behaviours in a neutral and transparent manner in which they are no longer able to control the situation or conversation.

Courage and timing

For those with less courage in the heat of the moment, I can recommend the strategy of 'setting the scene'. Bring up the topic at a calm time, when both of you are thinking about something else, or watching television. Feel free to turn to your partner and say, 'Hey, there is something big that I need to talk to you about sometime in the coming days. It has been on my mind for a while, and I need to get it off my chest. Is there a time when we can chat about this and work through this in the coming day or two, please?'

Usually, if the other person is watching television, they are not emotionally on guard, and so they can possibly be a little more approachable to setting the scene. Remember, all you are asking is for them to consider setting some time aside to talk to you about it in the coming days. Your purpose is to let them know you have something big to discuss, and you are hoping to have their calm attentiveness when they are ready to work through this with you.

If your partner is considerate and has priorities on the health and wellbeing of the relationship, then he or she will make time. In fact, they may even stop the movie or television, and say, 'Sure, let's talk about it now, if that helps'.

In an ideal world, this is great, and for couples that have a relatively healthy relationship already, this can work really well.

If your relationship is already under enormous strain, then use this strategy to address very minor issues. Once the partner feels that they are not ambushed with 'The Meaning of Life' every time you open a conversation, then they will feel comfortable engaging in this process more readily next time. Use a gradual-staged engaging process to gently address slightly larger or more important decisions next time and build from there.

If your partner is the 'Driver' and you are particularly anxious when you need to have serious discussions with them, I suggest you ask them if they can assist you on something that you know they would love to help you with, as it's something in their field of expertise. Strong leaders love to do what they do best, and that is *lead*.

Give them encouragement to open up and you will find a better response next time. Give loads of appreciation for your partner's time and input at the end of any difficult conversation. It is not easy, for either of you, but if you give appreciation, kindness and support, then they will feel more at ease for the next time you need to talk.

The good, bad and ugly

In the process of whatever personal journey you are on, there will be experiences that you will come across that are designed to challenge you as a person. I love these experiences, and have had my fair share of them too. Actually, if I think about it, I hate them too.

Challenging experiences are designed to test us to the core of who we are. Life is usually difficult, stressful and disappointing during these times. Sometimes the challenging experience can last several years, or at least a lot longer than we really want it to. I call them 'character-building experiences'. These are the experiences that will leave you forever changed as a person.

While we can talk about the good experiences, the fun ones, and the warm and fuzzy ones, they are too easy, and generally we have fun and enjoy these times. The 'ugly' experiences usually imprint themselves on our memories for years and rarely leave us easily, if at all.

Sharing your childhood stories and histories together, and talking about your lives growing up, helps both of you to understand what motivates you and drives you to do the things you do. It quantifies your beliefs and values. Knowing where you came from helps you to formulate whether you want to follow the same path as your parents have done, or forge a different one.

Sharing those parts of your own upbringing with your partner helps you to engage with each other's personal journeys and find similarities or maybe complementary opposite tales. You will begin to see why you have come together, and what strengths and characteristics you are forming that make your relationship and connection so strong together.

Now is the perfect time for you to speak up for your adult self and address the past experiences that you may not have fully dealt with yet. Through this process, support your partner, as they will be your support when it is your turn too.

The tough life

I know some really beautiful people who are genuine, heartfelt and wonderful people. For some reason though, which I can't understand or explain why, they seem to receive a lot of bad luck, or maybe there are just tragic things that happen for them more than other people.

Some of my dear friends and clients have lost their homes, businesses, and millions of dollars of assets through natural disaster, floods, fire and the like. There are friends of mine who have lost children and close family members through car accidents. The shear pain of loss that I have watched them go through brings tears to my eyes.

Some really close friends who have lost a lot over the duration of their business and marriage together are by far the most resilient people I have ever come across. They show up every day, and they try and stay positive, but you can tell that the burdens weigh heavily and will eventually take there toll on their health and wellbeing.

There will be times when one of you needs to bring the balance back, for example, by swinging the pendulum back to the middle when it has gone too far towards the 'too much work' side. However, be careful not to swing it to the 'too lazy' side, but somewhere in the middle is good. You must be able to have a weekend, or a holiday – a break of some kind at regular intervals. These things help you both to weather the storms together.

Weathering the storm together is important. You must share in the ups and downs, knowing that the boat carries both of you. There is no point in creating mutiny on the high seas, because you need all hands on deck to get safely back to shore. There is great strength in solidifying your relationship through the shared battleground. Be prepared for some losses along the way though, as there will be good times and bad times – you just need to ride the bad ones out. Support each other and hold on tight together.

Don't lay blame for the weather or things that neither of you can control. Each person has his or her own journey, but you also have a combined journey together.

Find strength in numbers and bring about greater kinship by sharing problems with the view of finding better solutions.

Communicate your fears and concerns, and share your best ideas and resolutions. Help each other through the tough decisions and emotional scars that will no doubt happen along the way. This journey is not always perfect – you are, after all, only human. You do the best you can with what you know at the time.

Ten minutes of 100% focus

When was the last time you were able to sit down by yourself, in peace and quiet, with no disturbances? For many busy people this is a rare thing; in fact, you probably can't even recall the last time you had some time off.

How good does it feel when you eventually do get some time for yourself? For me, I love sitting by the water, just myself alone, and taking time to recharge. I can think without someone distracting me, or interrupting my thoughts, and it is so amazingly refreshing.

For others, being alone and silent is extremely scary, as that is usually when you catch up with yourself, and all the important issues that you have successfully ignored come rushing into your mind. Mostly, someone who is scared of being alone will ensure that this doesn't happen by busying themselves with activities, sound, distractions or entertainment.

If you don't set time aside for yourself, then how can it be possible to have the energy to set time aside for your partner? You could spend every waking moment together, but still live miles apart on the inside. Many couples who live and work together have heaps of *quantity* time, and yet surprisingly little *quality* time.

The quality of your relationship comes down to something very simple; however, not many couples remember to make this a priority in their relationship. All it takes is ten minutes of your time. Of the 86,400 seconds of every day, it only requires 600 of those seconds to stop and actually pay attention to your partner?

Let me show you the difference it makes.

The power of ten minutes a day with my children

I have two daughters who are only 17 and a half months difference in age. As they grew up, one always was in the shadow of the other, as siblings are, and because they were close in age, both girls always seemed to compete for my attention.

When they were about ten and eleven, as a single parent, I had only myself to split across both children, and so I made a deal with each of them. I would give them ten minutes of my exclusive time every day. They each had to wait in their separate rooms until it was their turn, and neither child could disrupt the other child's time. They could play by themselves until I came to their room, and then they would have my 100% undivided attention.

During this time, I would look my children directly in their eyes. They would know that I was only focusing 100% on them, and not on my phone or laptop. I wasn't distracted thinking about something else, like work or dinner, and it was all about them for a whole ten minutes.

I wouldn't use that time to tell them rules or instructions, as it would be only their time to speak. They could talk about anything they wanted to. I would stay silent for that time (interacting and responding of course), and I would intently listen to them, making sure not to initiate my own agenda in the conversation. It was *their* time.

What this exercise did was confirm to each of my children, separately, that they were highly important in my life, and that I valued them as individuals. I wanted to spend time with them, and I wanted to *really* listen to them.

They responded so positively to this deal, and each child respected the other child's private time. No private conversations were discussed outside the room, as it was their safe place with my fullest attention.

This may sound like a simple exercise, and yet not that many people do this.

The secret to 'love'

Did you want to know the secret to showing your partner how much you truly love them? Look your partner directly in the eyes and hold eye contact for at least one minute. Stay silent and smile lovingly at them. Don't look down, get distracted by something, or look away. And give them the chance to speak about anything they want.

Be present in that moment and just listen to them – there's no need to fix any problems or come up with any solutions for them. Just let them speak. Even if you do this for just a few minutes a day, let it be a time when it is all about *them*. In fact, even five minutes a day is more than most people get. If you want to learn how to keep the relationship and romance alive, this is it.

Remember that you are going for transparency, respect, personal truth or alignment, and most of all, *acceptance* of the other person for who they are. You don't have to like what they say, or agree with anything, as this time is about *them*, not you. All you have to do is listen.

SECTION FIVE

Instead of worrying about what
you cannot control, shift your
energy to what you can create.

Roy T. Bennett

COOPERATION

Let's now spend some time taking stock of where you are.

By now you have covered off clarity around who you and your partner are as individuals and together in life and business. Once you have established the foundations to your relationship, you then explored the commitment levels that you each bring to your life journey together. Engaging in strong commitment – both in attitude and ability – to your joint futures, you have to naturally increase and enhance your communication skills.

Now, through effective communication and the solid foundations of who you are and where you are going together, you can begin to apply these strategies to your business, through 'cooperation'.

Cooperation is the *willingness* or act of working together for a common purpose or benefit, which is where couples in business really demonstrate their attitude towards creating that perfect future together.

Applying the practical and tangible aspects of your relationship forces you to get along and make things work, even when you may not 'feel the love' or really enjoy the process. You will probably sometimes find that you engage reluctantly with some of the business tasks at hand, in order to just get through your workload, or at least to ensure that the proverbial boat doesn't sink.

And cooperating with your partner may mean that you are not necessarily always doing what you particularly love or are passionate about, and yet you acknowledge that the overall objective is one for the improvement of your combined family and future.

There are, however, parts to this process that we have to be aware of. It is not always about a full sacrifice of ourselves for the sake of someone else's wellbeing. There may be times when we want to jump in and help, but that can also become detrimental to the other person's journey of learning and growing.

This section will provide guidance to couples that want to gain deeper understanding into the need for working out the business roles and responsibilities, and separating them from the roles in their personal lives.

Self-directed leadership

Cooperating in the home and the business allows couples to effectively set clear boundaries surrounding their different roles and responsibilities in both of these areas. 'Self-directed leadership' strategies that can help you cooperate better include recognising the importance of having systems, processes, limits, and 'safe words' when one person has reached their maximum.

Self-directed leadership is also about having the foresight to play out the consequences before taking action. For example, a person may feel like they want to go and rob a bank to solve their money stresses, but they choose not to because the consequence is highly likely to be jail time.

While not every decision or action is that extreme, there are always repercussions to any action taken. Your job as business owners is to ensure you build a great business that has loyal hardworking team members, an enjoyable working environment, and the ability for trust and delegation to allow you both to have a holiday without the place burning down while you are away.

Systemising the business

What is more important – being happy at home, or being happy in the business? The answer for most couples in business together is both. Each aspect is as important as the other. From the ups and downs in your personal relationship, you have to be able to *work* in harmony.

You and your partner each have a different set of skills to bring to the business. Some of you may be more creative and artistic, while others may be more detailed or technically minded. Some of you may have great organisation skills, and others are better at following the systems already laid in front of us.

Share your skills

Set the roles and responsibilities within your business together. Have discussions between yourselves and outline who will do what tasks in the business. Without clear roles and responsibilities, there is confusion around who takes the burden for things when something is not done. Only then, will you clearly know who the person is who is not playing their part. Remember, you are both in the journey together, and so without your combined efforts, the fabric of your future starts to disintegrate and fall apart.

One of the most frustrating things that can cause innumerable arguments between couples is when things go wrong inside the business. Let's face it, if we have a great relationship outside of the business, where we are on holiday, or relaxing without the extra stress, the only thing that could really muck it up is something that goes wrong with our financial security or stability within the business.

Because the business is your primary source of income, having the business functioning smoothly is your primary goal to ensure your family's needs are met. You want everything to be working well in the business, and then that makes your home life easier as well.

The family business model

The reality for many family-owned businesses is that they are just that – family. You may even often sacrifice the need for creating proper systems and structures within your business because, after all, it's just the two of you – so why do you need intricate processes? You both know what needs to be done, and so you don't document things properly. It kind of all just happens around you.

There are a great many benefits to having proper systems and documented procedures. Firstly, it provides clarity on each person's roles and responsibilities, which we discussed earlier, and that is extremely important. However, even more important that this is that it provides clarity on the 'work flow process'. How do you process your customer requests, or products and services that you provide, which generate your income?

Within all businesses, there are 'checkpoints' where one person checks the other person's work. It may be done at the front counter, or it may be at a dispatch bench, or a point where one person takes over the job process from another person.

Whatever is required to allow the product or service to flow, there will be areas that you can spot check in your business.

Let me ask you a question – how good is your business?

Another aspect of the myriad of services that my business provides for small businesses is that I also offer business coaching for family-run businesses. I create tools and strategies for each individual business model based around the specific requirements that each workplace requires. Having completed a degree in Business and Commerce, majoring in marketing and management, I am able to combine real-life business experience with the leading-edge strategies from a standard of business excellence across all areas of any industry.

Having built my consulting business over the past 12 years, we apply realistic expectations and results around the workplace structures that are essential for any successful business. We have combined workshops and programs to assist couples in strengthening their relationship foundations with the view to ensure that they build a successful business together.

I sometimes ask my clients for a list of the customers they have served in the past ten days, and then I call some of those clients. The feedback and responses are then presented as part of the coaching process for my clients to work through.

Now, if I was to randomly call five of your customers, and four of them had average experiences, how would you feel about your business? This might make you feel apprehensive about your businesses success; however, the feedback is extremely valuable in order to help you improve your business. This improvement could be achieved by giving your staff more training, or rewriting a specific sales script, or even looking for a better quality supplier. Whatever the situation, at least you know what needs improving, and you can take the necessary steps towards making these improvements.

What if I called five of them and four people gave raving reviews – how would you feel about your business then? Pretty good, I bet!

Creating systems

Everything inside the business can be *fixed* by creating a great 'system'.

Firstly, write down each section of the business. For each section, list the tasks and duties for each part of the process. For each task, write down a list of items that are required to complete each task properly. And then test this document by asking someone who has never done that job before, or who doesn't know your business, to read it. If they can understand what you are explaining, then it a good system. See if they can follow your written instructions and complete the required tasks

For staff members, have a list of duties that they are required to complete. Make a list of things that you can measure their performance with. For example, do they turn up to work on time? Are their uniforms clean? Do they make mistakes? Do they follow company procedures properly? Are they safe in the workplace? These will be yes/no types of measurements, which work well. With this list, you can then set systems to measure the performance of almost anything you want in your business.

Systems are imperative to ensure that orders don't get lost, customers receive product on time, and customer service levels are maintained. Measurements for business can be set to make sure you are aware of any poor customer experiences that are being received. Everything needs to have a proper flow, which makes your business transactions smooth and efficient.

Quality assurance checkpoints

Every business needs to have some way of checking that the ongoing quality of product or service is up to standard. There has to be some way of ensuring that every product consistently meets the required standards, and that each customer service experience is the same for every sale, every time. This is called 'quality assurance'.

However, it would be extremely time-consuming and commercially unviable to check every single item before it went out the door, and so 'checkpoints' have to be put in place within the business.

'Why did the match company go out of business? Because they tested every match they made.' This is a typical example of how unviable it would be to test every product, because after the match is lit, it is of no further use. This is a classic case of 'overdoing' quality assurance, and while quality assurance is extremely important for your business, you don't want it to be the destruction of your business.

So how much quality assurance do you need? What benefits should quality assurance have *for* your business?

The purpose behind ensuring and maintaining a desired level of service or standards comes down to a very simple and yet often overlooked foundation to business success, and that is 'consistency'.

McDonald's has been a successful business model – even though there are plenty of other businesses that make a better hamburger – because of its consistency.

Consistency is the key to the success of business branding.

So why is consistency important? It's because every customer then knows what to expect when they shop with you and your business, and if it's a good experience for them, they will keep coming back to you, or at least recommend you to others. If their experience varies from transaction to transaction, the customer is going to be unsure about taking a risk on what sort of product or service quality they will get next time, and they may therefore not use your business.

Human beings are creatures of habit, and we like to live mostly within our comfort zone. Having a consistent product or service helps a customer buy from a business that fulfils their need within their comfort zone.

Quality assurance processes are primarily there to ensure the customer's expectations are met with some form of consistency and structure. To minimise mistakes or faults within the flow, your business needs to have 'quality assurance checkpoints' in place. These could be at the beginning, middle and end of the production line.

Check products that go out the door at random. This is generally called 'spot checking'. Large manufacturing plants often select 2–5% of the product at random, to check the quality and performance. Sometimes this is visual, while other products require closer examination.

What checkpoints can you create in your business to ensure your product or service is maintaining a high standard of excellence?

Setting these systems up may seem like a big effort; however, as your business grows, it will become much easier to manage and keep a track of. Use spot checks and quality checklists to make your business life run smoothly.

Creating documents

If you are unsure on how to go about doing this, there are plenty of resources available; however, a simple table on a Word Document or an Excel Spreadsheet has survived many a true test of time.

Firstly, all you need to do is simply list all the things you want to know about your business in order to keep track of its success. For example, you may want to see a 'Business Productivity Checklist'. Or maybe you need to keep a track of the 'number of enquiries' you get per day. If you need to get more than five a day, and you do, then you know that you are on track. If you don't get more than five, then perhaps you need to look into why you didn't and work out a way to make sure you can reach your targets in the future.

Other things that may be important to know could include: 'number of sales'; 'sales in dollars per week'; 'staff sick leave'< (less than) 1 day per month; 'number of call backs'< (less than) 1 per month; 'number of new customers'. Whatever you wish to track in your business, it can be done simply and easily with a one-page document or spreadsheet table.

The key is to make your systems easy to use. Make any system traceable and measureable. Keep all systems organised in numerical or chronological order. And have clear instructions on using the systems, and don't allow shortcuts, as this can create more hassle down the road.

Following the system

Everyone is human, and everyone make mistakes, so you need to state very clearly when your partner (or staff member) does *not* follow the wonderful and comprehensive systems that you have created inside your business.

I am not going to lie to you and tell you that it is all rosy and smooth sailing once you have created the business systems, but hopefully, with what you have learnt so far in this book, you know how to address issues if people don't follow the systems.

Creating systems allows you to know where you are in the cycle. Having budgets is a great system that you can follow in order to keep yourselves and your business flowing effortlessly.

Everything can be created into a system; however, the effectiveness of these systems comes down to the responsibility of both people in the relationship and the business to *follow* those systems. Try not to deviate from them too often or too far. In fact the closer that you stick to the systems, the better your business shall be. In an ideal world, I would say that under no circumstances should you deviate from the system.

Roles and responsibilities

Create a list of skills that each person can use to contribute to the business. Set clear guidelines as to what each person can do, and what responsibilities they can take on within the business.

Some partners may have a smaller role that seems simple and easy, while the other person may feel like they are carrying the entire load and weight of the whole business on their shoulders. So ensure you make things even and equitable, or at least you both know why one partner might not take on as much as the other (perhaps they take on more responsibility in the home, as discussed previously). It is easy to become overwhelmed in all roles, and this is where the support from each partner is extremely important.

Differences in the amount of workload you both take on may also be due to a personality trait – one of you might just naturally take on everything and can't let go of any of their responsibilities.

If you feel that you or your partner suffer from this, try to relax and let other people take responsibility for things in the business as well. I know that this is difficult to do at times, but if your partner is the more 'chilled one', then they are there to teach you that it is okay to let go, even just a little bit.

Hiring staff

Make sure that you have a good understanding of what your business needs are in the form of staff, before you make the decision to hire anyone. Staff can help or greatly hinder your business. Write a list of duties that you want them to do. Try not to make the mistake of putting three or four different jobs into the one role, as it can be confusing for your applicant, as well as frustrating and expensive for you to find the ideal candidate.

Also recommended when hiring staff is to make sure you also select the type of personality fit that works best with the role, as well as within your 'company culture'. For example, if you are a law firm and need analytical, detailed, quiet and intelligent people to do research for you, then it is no use hiring someone bubbly, outgoing, chatty and expressive. They will not only disrupt your office with noise and loud laughter, they will not be detailed enough in their research because of a lack of analytical ability.

For the same reason, if you are running a restaurant, it is no good putting a very shy, quiet, or slow person with limited social skills on the front counter for receiving customer orders. They are best suited to being in the back helping in the kitchen or in some other area that does not require them to be extroverted. It is important to carefully select and know what best suits your business before you hire anyone to assist.

Work-free zones

There needs to be a place at home where there is 'no work talk' allowed.

I realise that the business is your 'baby', and without both of your efforts, the baby would die. It is ridiculous to think that separating work from home and home from work is an absolutely achievable goal. One of you will inevitably be thinking, planning, pondering, or arranging what to do in the business, while you are preparing a meal at home, or something on the television prompts a thoughtful discussion on how to approach a current work challenge.

In fact, talking about work at home on a limited basis can be a good thing, as you will not have 'work' distractions and can have full and frank discussions about plans for the future. It is recommended though that there be a ritual or process whenever work talk needs to be done. Sit at the desk or in a separate work office space that you can both discuss, plan and document what you would like to accomplish.

However, there also needs to be an area where work is not discussed. Each of you should become accountable to the other person when together in this space, and ensure that it is a sacred and respected 'work free zone'. For my husband and I, it is our outdoor spa area, where we can relax and enjoy any type of discussion, as long as it does not involve work. For some couples this forces them to find topics or areas of interest separate to the workplace, and it allows for a balance between work life and home life.

There is a fantastic book written by Australia's number one best-selling business author, Andrew Griffiths, called *101 Ways to Have a Business and a Life*. If you are short of ideas on how to rebalance your business and home life, this book is highly recommended for reigniting the creative juices on what things need attention and change for the benefit of yourself, your relationship, your workspace and home life[10]. It's well worth applying these strategies to create balance, harmony and fulfilment in your life.

---

10 Griffiths, A 2007, *101 Ways to Have a Business and a Life*, Allen and Unwin Publishers, Australia.

Working together without conflict

For any effective business, government or military exercise to work well, there has to be leaders and supporters. By nature we cannot have two leaders pulling in different directions. Like in families where the children play one parent against the other, the same is true in a business where the couple works together actively on a daily basis and manage staff.

A clear pathway of leadership and authority has to be established, even for the purpose of maintaining a united front inside the business. After-hour discussions can be had away from the staff, as you don't want your business to represent the 'art of war' through dividing and conquering.

Conflict at work

During any conflict, there are times to stand your ground, and there are times to compromise. There will be give and take in all negotiations and mediation situations where conflict is present and both people will not back down. Having clear roles and responsibilities helps to separate decision-making lines between two people in business. For example, when it comes to technical decisions, my husband makes these, but when it comes to money or business strategy decisions, it is my responsibility.

For couples in business, having conflict is a natural and frequent part of working and living together. It is important for couples to have great strategies around managing negotiation and mediation between themselves. Having emotional connections will also naturally increase the stress levels between the two people, as well as inviting the opportunity to switch off and totally ignore what the other person is asking of you.

Exchanging energy

We are all have our own unique energy. Without having an opportunity to refill our own energy, the only other way to obtain a boost is to take it from someone else. Have you ever noticed how some people make us feel great, while others drain us and leave us feeling emotionally spent?

Nothing is more true that during an argument. One person leaves the room feeling deflated, exhausted and overall beaten, while the other person skips out of the room on cloud nine feeling euphoric, almost dizzy with excitement that they have won the battle of whits.

This exact scenario is what happens when one person takes energy from the other person. The person left feeling drained is exactly that – drained of energy. In fact, they will probably go and lie down after a short time, and it may take several hours to recover. Failing that, they will most likely seek out a friend, someone who gives them the most solace and comfort, to help replace the 'lost' or 'stolen' energy that the initial person took from them.

Lifting each other up

Often, when my children are feeling down or low, they will come to me for a hug, and I will close my eyes, wrap my arms around them and imagine filling them up with all the love a mother can muster. Within minutes they are feeling better again, smiling, laughing, and they are back to their normal self.

This is a pattern – a law of life, if you will. We have energy in our bodies that provides life and sustenance to others. We can either give it freely, or we can have it stolen, or taken against our will, such as when we are 'losing' an argument. The other person can take it purely by outwitting us with logic, or by creating more dominance and thereby inciting our negative emotions of fear, guilt or rejection.

Don't make it personal

You must have the facts or the correct information to rely upon when in an argument. Most arguments are heated and emotional. Remember that whenever someone is emotional, they are out of balance with perspectives. Staying in balance will allow you to remain connected with yourself. When you are connected, there will be things that the other person says that will seem odd to you. For some reason, the comments or statements will just 'not sit right'.

It is then imperative to gently question the reason as to why your partner is making sweeping and broad-stroke statements that are intended to sting or disorientate you. So remain calm and unemotional, but think logically. Ask questions of the other person and get their attention enough to stop them from trying to steal your energy. Having someone thinking about their own statements, rather than accepting whatever is said must be true, will give you a chance to solidify your protective energy field and rebalance yourself enough to hopefully calm any disturbance between you.

Speak calmly and establish their reason for being upset. They might be feeling low themselves in order to seek energy from you in the first place. Find out what is really bothering them, and then give each other a loving hug in order to transfer, by choice, your love, energy and support to your partner in a healthy and positive way. The trick is not to take it personally, nor make it personal.

Effective teamwork

My husband noticed how well we work together when we first met by the way we jointly cooked our first meal together. In a very small space of the kitchen, we both went about our separate roles, without fuss, not bumping into each other, and we coordinated the timing of the meal to be ready at the same time.

By the time I had finished serving the dinner on plates and had it ready at the dinner table, he had done all the dishes and wiped up the mess in the kitchen so we could both sit down and enjoy our meal together. It was absolutely amazing that he even realised this, because I didn't even think twice about how we synchronised our positions or use of cooking equipment, but he noticed.

Teamwork is about creating a smooth and synchronised transition between each person working together on a particular task.

Synchronising ourselves is what my husband and I do well together whenever we work. It is almost as if we can predict each other's next move, and we have the tools ready, or the mat out ready. While there is a certain amount of intuition about what your partner needs next, it is not about 'mind-reading' their next move.

The simple answer to how to work effectively as a team comes down to three things:
- **Process** – Knowledge of what needs to happen.
- **Anticipation** – Anticipating the next steps or requirements.
- **Transition** – Smooth and seamless exchange to continued progress.

For example, you would generally know when your partner was about to step out of the shower if you were in the bathroom at the same time. An indicator would be that they turn the shower off and stop the water from flowing. You also know that once a shower is turned off and complete, you would need to open the door and step out into the bathroom, pick up your towel and start drying yourself off. Seems logical enough.

Because you already know the process of showering, then it is easy to anticipate the next step. You can position yourself, outside the shower, with enough room to move backwards when your partner exits, and perhaps hold the towel out for them because you know they will need it to dry off. The process happens as you predict.

There, you have 'teamwork'!

Applying teamwork at work

While not every process is as simple as this example, there are greater opportunities to learn little things that may be helpful to your partner. Shine a light into a dark space if they are trying to work with both hands and can't hold a torch themselves. Have the screwdriver or hammer ready when they are working around the house. Maybe pour your partner a drink while they are coming in the front door from the office, or if you arrive together, one put the kettle on, while the other person feeds the dog or baths the children.

Most people can have a relatively good level of teamwork; however, some tasks are a lot harder than day-to-day living. Some things, I just don't understand and so I can't help in any way possible. Sometimes I have no clue as to what my husband wants or needs to help him complete a particular task. In these instances, teamwork may be as simple as staying well out of the way, and letting your partner get on with the job.

Wherever you see two people struggling to get things done, you know that their teamwork needs a lot of practice. The best way to measure if you have good teamwork is by the results – the results of your combined efforts to work fast and efficiently, as well as how accurately and concisely you achieve an outcome.

Take a moment to think about how well you and your partner work together. Are you *effective* in what you do, or are there mistakes and gaps in the finished product? Are you both *efficient*, or does a particular job seem to take much longer than it should?

What are some past projects you have worked on together, and what are the results? Why do you feel those results are there? What could have been done to improve the teamwork between you and your partner that would have given a better result?

Teamwork takes practice. It also takes communication between the two of you. Without proper communication, you will not work well together in any situation. I don't mean that you should be *talking* throughout the project. I mean that you should both discuss – communicate and organise – the project beforehand, arrange who does what, and then set about doing your tasks and assisting wherever needed to help your partner achieve their tasks as well. That is good teamwork.

Your journey together is not a competition to see who wins or who finishes first. Just like a three-legged race at the fair, the person who gets to the finish line first but left their partner behind in the race is not the winner.

Teamwork is one of the most important foundations when working together, and it can define who you are as individuals and what level of commitment you have to each other. From there you can build on teamwork through 'communication', 'cooperation', and sharing your vision through 'collaboration'. This will build your family's successful future in the most effective and efficient way possible.

Being responsible – accepting that we all make mistakes / Being accountable – taking action

In your home life and business life, there will be ups and downs, mistakes and wins, rewards and struggles – emotionally, financially, physically and spiritually. I have counselled enough businesses and couples in business to know that there are times when you will feel like giving up, and there will be many times when you feel like blaming each other.

So let's look at how you can overcome these particular times.

Maintaining balance at work and in the relationship

Breanne and Kevin have been together for eleven years and have been running a plumbing business together for eight years.

Breanne said to me, 'The only reason I stopped the credit card was because he went out last week and spent money on something we couldn't afford.'

Kevin replied with, 'I only did that because you have been so grumpy. We needed some extra toolboxes and other stuff. Anyway, why should I have to justify what goes on here?'

'I can't make payments out of thin air,' Breanne commented back.

I could see that we were getting nowhere with this conversation, so I called a 'time out'.

I then explained to them that each person is intertwined with the other. It is part of being in a relationship. When one pulls one way, then the other person has to follow.

And then to maintain balance, the other person has to pull back again. No matter what happens, because the both of you are in a relationship, there will always be pulling that will affect your partner.

So ultimately you have to deal with your issues separately.

I told them both to go back and disarm their 'triggers'. Then when they got back together again to discuss the issue, they would not intentionally or deliberately do things that would create waves in the business or in the relationship.

Actions and consequences

Remember that you have no control over what someone else does or does not do. You can, however, adjust whether you allow that person to bother you. Once you can understand the processes and how this affects your ability to work together, then you can see things for what they are. You can more easily deal with your own 'triggers', if you are clear on where your boundaries and issues start and stop, and then you might see that the problem actually belongs with the other person.

The actions of each person inside the business and inside the relationship will automatically affect their partner. No one person is on the journey alone, as you are both in it together. You can either work together to make a great and successful future, or you can quietly sabotage the process.

Rather than laying blame for mistakes, work together to find a solution. The platform for your relationship should not be about who can be in control, or about competitiveness – your relationship with your partner should be about *togetherness*.

Couples in healthy relationships support each other when they are low. If one partner has had a bad day, the other partner will lift them up. I think the happier relationships are those couples that provide loving support to one another, and those who accept each other's faults and shortcomings but love each other regardless.

Listen to advice from others

My most valuable lesson in business came about when I was about 25 years old. I had started my own business in direct selling homewares and linens. I put my whole heart and soul into that business, and my level of excitement and enthusiasm had never been so high. I was extremely proud of my achievements when I created this business. It was my first solo business, and I invested a great deal of money in order to promote it at an exhibition. For anyone who has been to an organised event, it can cost thousands of dollars just for two or three days in front of potential customers.

I stood proudly, fronting my stall for the first two days. I had brought in a beautiful bedroom suite and set it up perfectly. I had a fantastic offer of an entire linen collection for a winning customer who entered the draw, and I was so overwhelmed with enthusiasm for the business as a whole. The only problem was that I didn't get the response that I was hoping for.

About half way through the final day of the exhibition, one guy from the neighbouring stall came over and said to me, 'I'm sorry, but I can't let you do this to yourself anymore. I have to tell you something.'

I looked at him eagerly, wondering what I was doing wrong.

He then said, 'You have stood proudly in front of your stall for the past two days, but no one can actually get into the stall.' He politely explained that my positioning was blocking potential customers from going into the stand and having a look around. I was the one stopping them from entering my business space and completing the entry forms for the competition!

I will never forget that moment as long as I live.

I then stood back and watched people pour into my display area to assess my wares and to also write their names on my competition entry forms. This lovely man showed me something that was so simple to do, and yet also so simple to stuff up! I had absolutely no idea that I had been blocking my own success, as I was too close to see my own mistakes.

There is great value in life lessons, and there is even more value in those people who are willing to help support you through the learning of those lessons.

I now provide business coaching and mentoring support to family businesses because I have a deep desire to help them. I love supporting people in rekindling their desire for their business, and helping them become the best they can be for themselves and each other.

SECTION SIX

Go confidently in the direction
of your dreams!
Live the life you've imagined.

Henry David Thoreau

COLLABORATION

'Collaboration' is the combined forces that work seamlessly together to synchronise your efforts and increase your efficiency and effectiveness within the business, and ultimately bring about greater success of your business.

Collaboration also means jointly working together even though you may disagree on things; however, you are both still willing to make the best of any situation. You work closely with your partner to create the reality of your shared or common visions. You are co-producers of the successful outcomes that bring about your shared lives together.

So far you have learnt that you each have different perspectives. You have accepted each other's differences and still choose to work together for the common good – to work with one another on a joint project.

Collaboration means to participate, do business with, to co-produce something fantastic together.

Now that you have learnt to cooperate with each other, you can finally create great visions for your future. You have the makings of a great team. You can now pull together in the same direction and magnify your combined efforts in order to create magic.

It's time to open the doors to your success and receive the joint fruits of your labour in your business so that you can enjoy each other's company and admire the hard work you have done to get you to this point.

You are now an effective team, and with a few tweaks, you can call yourselves a 'Peak Performance Team' or 'Dynamic Duo'. This section discusses the finer points to collaboration that are essential for any successful couple in business together.

Once a couple can discuss anything, and they know what is required and have a brilliant ability to work together, the final piece of the puzzle becomes clear. The energy, passion and vision that two people bring to a business are incredibly powerful. Collaboration brings about the ultimate goal, allowing couples to recognise the pathway forward.

Creating common visions

Whatever happens within your relationship, it is important that you both share your visions, goals, hopes and dreams for your respective futures. What is 'success' and what does it mean to each of you both? Talk regularly about the things that you want, and why you may want those things. Without checking in daily or weekly with your partner, the relationship could take a diverging pathway and catch you both off guard.

Clarify more specifically on what you want the business to provide for you both. What sort of target income are you seeking, and how is this going to be achieved together? Write down in your business plan the things that you are both agreeing on. Even come up with the 'pros' and 'cons' of each opportunity. This will create hours of planning, discussion, organisation and management of the business that you can both work on together.

However, remember this should be a fun and enjoyable time together. It's like planning a holiday, where you explore possibilities, dream of the destination and plan the logistics surrounding your vacation. Planning your business growth and future can provide similar excitement as you explore options, dream of the destination, and discuss the logistics on getting you to that ultimate vision.

Your dream business model

Imagine I gave you a 1000-piece Jigsaw puzzle. How would you begin to go about doing the jigsaw puzzle? Most people would start with the four corners, and they would pull out the four individual pieces within that jigsaw puzzle that have two perfectly flat sides. Then they would separate all the edgy bits, the pieces that have at least one perfectly flat side.

Next, they would set those to one side and start creating the boundaries and borders of the puzzle picture. Constantly referring back to the front cover of the box that shows them the full picture completely, they would separate the colours and group the pieces of the puzzle images together – blue for the sky, green for the grass, brown and reds for the autumn trees and the buildings. They would start to see the picture forming as they worked on putting all the pieces together.

You take the same approach with your *business*, as you have in your combined minds what the perfect completed picture is supposed to look like. Without this ultimate 'vision', you have no idea where your pieces of the business jigsaw puzzle will fit. You could come across some great bargains, but without the full and completed picture, you have no idea about where these great bargains will fit into your store, or your business model.

As long as you have a complete picture, you can see where things are supposed to go, and you can match your current business with the ideal business image. It's exactly the same as matching your puzzle pieces to the picture on the front of the box. Only then can you find any gaps or holes in your business and fill them properly.

Confused business owners

So what would happen if there were some problems with your jigsaw puzzle? What if there were 100 randomly selected pieces of the jigsaw puzzle missing from your box? You are going to have an incomplete picture, one with lots of holes, probably at the most critical points in the picture. This is the same as with your business. When you miss out parts of a system, holes tend to show up in your business.

What happens if there is 150 pieces inside the puzzle box that actually belong to a completely different puzzle? There will be confusion as you try to put the puzzle together with pieces that just do not match, nor belong with your currently designed puzzle. What would happen to your business if you were to put pieces together that just did not belong?

I often look at stores that have random themes of stock without consistency or flow. Very little thought has obviously been put into the business planning or project, and very often the store is just a collection of things that an individual would find enjoyable, but the majority of things are of little use to a specific target market.

Having a good product or service that fills a great need for customers is the perfect start to ensuring your business planning has been executed correctly. Knowing your target market and being able to effectively communicate with them is essential to ensuring the long-term survivability and sustainability of your business together.

Using both minds and hearts in your business is what will strengthen the foundations from which you create magic together. Build upon your business acumen and provide a continual learning process through which extra skills and strengths can be brought together in both your relationship and your business journey. There are opportunities for free learning of information through YouTube, or the internet. In fact, anything that you want to know more about will have millions of search results from around the world.

Without having to soak up a lifetime of information, answers should come together for you both within an hour of some targeted research and learning. Follow your instincts and be open to learning through synchronicity, and this shall help with bringing the answers to you sooner. Follow your gut. If you feel that something will help you learn what you need to, then take part in it. There are no right or wrong pathways, only choices and consequences.

For those who fear going down a pathway that might be a scam, then learn more about identifying and discerning people who may be there to take advantage of unsuspecting shoppers. If you want security in knowing the various types of people you are dealing with, find a provider that has a 'money-back guarantee' on their product or service.

Whatever your goal is together, you will find a way to make it happen; however, you must have a common goal, a joint vision of where you want to head on this journey. I often say to people in business that whenever you apply a force to drive the business, you need to make sure you are heading in the right direction. Make sure you have a good grip on the business. Seek support from business consultants and coaches to ensure you are making smart business decisions together.

Are you sure of the direction you both want to take? Your business will either be going through the roof, or through the floor, either way, your business is going in some direction.

Talk with each other. Discuss every aspect of what is going wrong in the business, as well as what is going really well. Don't just take the great stuff and minimise the not so great, because that will be the downfall of both in the end.

Assessing milestones and targets – rewarding yourselves

I remember watching the great motivational speaker Anthony Robbins one day. He was telling the audience about his 'golf' story. He had hired a golf professional to help him learn the art of golfing, and to work on perfecting his swing. The first day, he was going really well and was on target for his best ever golf score. Things were great.

The following morning he arrived on the green and started hitting golf balls, but they seemed to veer off into the sand, or into the bushes. He just couldn't seem to get it right. As he questioned his coach about this, the coach said, 'Just one millimetre'.

That was all.

The angle at which Anthony Robbins was hitting the ball was one millimetre off centre, and yet that caused the ball to go miles off course when the ball flew out over the fairway.

I think this is a really interesting analogy, and I often use it in my daily conversations with clients. Your business is functioning the way that it is because of your 'golf swing'. Perhaps, you don't play golf, but you can appreciate the assimilation. There may be things within your business that are 'almost' perfect, or maybe even 'almost' done. Whatever the results you are getting, it could just be a matter of tweaking a few minor adjustments in your understanding that can create a totally different result.

Your 'mindset' is the most powerful component to how your business functions, and for couples in business, the combined mindset on focusing your efforts together is truly an amazing and dynamic force.

Your ability to perceive and respond accordingly makes all the difference in the success or failure of your business. I usually find that nine times out of ten, if there is a problem in the business, it comes from the head space of the owner. Either they are not aware of the problems, or are part of creating problems within the business purely through a lack of understanding of the consequences of choices and decisions they make.

So ask yourself:
- How do you approach your clients, or your staff?
- How do you see your product or service?
- What lengths do you go to in order to recoup your money?
- Every action has our mindset behind the decisions we make.

Maximising the reward for effort

A fabulous way to reward yourselves is to plan a holiday. It is generally one of the most enjoyable things to look forward to. Even if you can't take much time 'off', get a 'business minder' for a couple of days, maybe even take the Friday off and have a long weekend. Whatever the situation, I am sure the business can cope without you both for a day or two.

Extended holidays

One of my clients came to me once with a question about how to make their holidays more enjoyable, as they were worried that they would spend too much time thinking about the business, and the time away seemed too short. His business was actually going really well, and they had plenty of money and were heading off for four weeks to go skiing in Aspen.

His concern was that he loved skiing, but even four weeks would go by too fast. He almost wanted to stay there forever, but he couldn't because he had to come back to his business.

I provided a strategy that I use for many of my 'short and sweet' holiday moments. Whenever I have only a few days to enjoy a break or holiday, I ensure I gain the most relaxation time for those short stays. I find myself a quiet place in the sunshine, either next to the pool, in a park, or by the beach, and I sit down and close my eyes. As I soak up the sunshine or atmosphere of wherever I am on holiday, I imagine that I am there for a year, not just three days.

For my client, I advised him to create an opportunity for a five-minute meditation, three to four times a day, for the first week. He had to ensure that he was present in the moment and imagine that he had an endless winter ahead of him. Nothing could drag him away, and there were no demands from his business at all. He had to allow his mind the fullness of fantasy and enjoyment of being there in the moment for a full year ahead.

The second week, I suggested that he combine the meditation to include a whole year of skiing in front of him, *and* a year already behind him. This helped to extend the relaxation time.

The final week, he had to imagine that he had been skiing there for many years, and that he was now ready to go home. This brought about fulfilment of a very complete experience.

Feel free to try this strategy, even during a one-day trip to the beach. Lay down in the sunshine and soak up the atmosphere of relaxation and rest. Allow yourself to stretch the concept of time across days, weeks, months and years if you want to.

Your mind is a powerful tool, and you are entitled to stretch the imagination as far as you want to. Use it to help with relaxing and making the most of your timeout. Make sure that you have no interruptions during this process, as it requires you to have full concentration of the enjoyment surrounding your relaxation time.

The best thing about your imagination is that you can imprint these memories and immerse yourself in the moment. Each person has the power of their imagination to recall the atmosphere and the feelings of enjoyment and sensations of any memory at a moment's notice. Lie back, relax and soak in the moments as much as you can, and thoroughly enjoy it.

Setting goals and stepping back

Have you ever gone to a football match where there were no goal posts? Which way would the teams play if there were no posts? How would they know where to score a try, or what way to run towards? How would the fans and spectators know who wins the game? The truth is, you wouldn't know. It would just be a bunch of people running all over the field with a ball. There would be no point or purpose.

The same happens in business. You have to have targets that allow you both to identify if you are on track or off track. You need to understand what is required to keep the business on track, and if it does go off track, how to turn it around.

Firstly, you have to ensure that your 'business systems' are in place. You have to have tight controls over the systems. Once the systems are in place, you can then make sure that everyone *follows* the systems. There has to be a clear pathway through each aspect of the business, which is explained to your team. That way they can carry out their jobs with ease.

Spot check the performance measurement criterion that is critical to the survival of your business. Allow yourself one hour per week to check in on all the performance measurements you need to feel comfortable the business is on track. Measure important things such as the number of sales, accounts payable, staff attendance, received money, profit and cash in the bank.

Having your business systems in place is even more important when you both go on holidays or are not in the office. Ensure you have all your systems running smoothly and for the benefit of your business before you leave to go away for an extended period of time.

Remote control business

Running a business is like lunging a horse. For those who are unfamiliar with this process, there is usually a horse in a round yard, and they have one rope that is connected to their halter, and the trainer or person stands in the centre of the ring. The horse is then given commands through the rope or reign, and the use of a lunge whip is there just to guide the horse for the instructions. The horse will turn, stop, go fast or slow, depending on the commands given by the person through the singular reign that is connecting the horse and person.

You and your partner, as business owners, need to be able to control your business through a singular reign or rope. It's even better if your business can function without you having to be 'on the horse', and all you need to do is just guide it from a distance without you having to actually do everything. If all you have to do is just give instructions to your team, knowing that they will follow those instructions, you can essentially allow your business to do the work and you can step back and relax more.

For this to happen effectively, you would firstly need to teach the 'horse' the commands and what the instructions mean. This means investing time into training your staff adequately. And you have to have proper systems in place and spot checks to maintain quality assurance and effectiveness of the business systems.

Building a successful business

You need to ensure there are great systems in place to make your business run at its optimum.

Essentially, your business needs three things:
- **Cash** – The business must be profitable on its own merits. If you are continually seeking more funding to support the business, you will eventually run out of money and go bankrupt.
- **Customers** – Without customers to purchase your product or service, you don't have a business, you have a hobby. If there are plenty of people who want your service or product but are not willing to pay for it, these are called free-loaders, and they will cause you to have no income.
- **Control** – Without having control over the business systems and processes, checkpoints, quality assurance, and all those

important aspects of keeping the business on track, the business will implode.

Increasing profits

Most clients that are struggling financially in their business often say, 'I just need more customers'. When I look into their business, they seem to have a steady flow of customers, and yet they are always in need of more money in the bank. It costs a business four times the amount to get a new customer, as it does to get repeat business by servicing an existing customer well.

So how can you increase your bank balance from the business you already have now?

Well, firstly, you have to understand the difference between cashflow and profit. Business owners can often confuse sales with profit, and it is not until they run out of money at the end of the month that they realise something is wrong.

Whatever business you are in right now, here are some things that you can implement immediately to increase your bottom line.

Here are four things you can do to increase your business profits, before you go looking for new customers:
1. Raise your prices, assuming that you are not already at the peak of what the market can possibly handle – generally a 10% increase in sales price will directly benefit your bottom line.

Depending on payment terms, this could still take two to three months for the profit to start showing in your bank account.

2. Increase your conversion rate – the number of enquiries that you can convert to actual purchases of your product or service. Changing or improving your sales scripting process or your customer experience processes can significantly increase your chances of the customer making a purchase from your business. It comes down to the wording, or the ability to walk the customer through the purchasing experience with you. Having skilled and well-trained staff is definitely helpful.
3. Create an increase in the dollars a customer spends by introducing packaging, bundling products or services, and up-selling, also known as 'value-adding'. You can place extra products or services together with a core product or service and increase the average sale price, but offer a discount for the combined purchase.
4. Increase the frequency of existing customers. The use of loyalty cards and special deals, bundling, or split packaging will get customers to come more frequently. There are opportunities to offer specific specials on certain days, different product specials, or have 'for a limited time' offers, and many other marketing strategies that will help to increase your current customer's buying habits.

After you have done the first four things, you should have a stronger and more profitable business position. From there, if you can handle more customers, only then do you need to go forth and seek new or more customers.

There are loads of tools and strategies that are available to assist business owners in refining and mastering the customer experience processes that will greatly increase the profitability and the success of their business. No person in business is alone; in fact, they even have a 'Turn-Around Management Committee' organisation that is filled with professionals that can help businesses in dire trouble. Check out the website www.turnaround.org.au for further information.

Mostly, for family-owned businesses, the benefit is that there are two of you. If one person needs to get work elsewhere for a short time to cover bills until you get through the next tough patch, then that may have to happen.

Alternatively, it could mean that one partner who is only working part time in the business may need to put in some extra hours in order to bring the business back on track. Whatever is needed, you will both pull together to improve your business.

Peak performance teams

When you see someone who is very successful in what they do, they are generally passionate and determined that their pathway is the best way to achieve what they want in life. The same goes in any business venture. As a couple running your business together, you both need passion and determination to make your business succeed.

The entire concept around collaboration is about both of you putting your energies into building a business and a relationship that is focused on what you both want to achieve together.

It is counter-productive if you have different visions, or different passions, or if one person is determined to make this a success, while the other person is 'merely interested'. To build a 'Peak Performance Team', and essentially become that 'Dynamic Duo' together, you both have to build the 'vision' of success around the business and the relationship.

Having clear visions of winning that tender, or gaining those new customers will help bring things into reality. Remember the 'law of attraction' – what you think about and visualise will be drawn nearer to you.

Ask yourselves:
- What is important to you both?
- What are your joint visions about your life and future together?
- Where do you want to be in two years, three years, or five years?
- Where do you want to live when you retire?

Each dream will become a reality the more you focus on them. As discussed earlier, whatever you focus on grows.

The key to being that 'Dynamic Duo in Business' is to start living out your goals and visions. Sit down and map the vision chart with your partner about the business, and your personal lives together.

Creating 'dream boards' or 'vision boards' together helps to surround yourselves with positive goals to work on for a successful future. As long as you are building something together, it may as well be as far as you can both reach.

Strive long and hard to reach your goals. Keep faith that you will eventually have that dream, as long as you both continue to pool your efforts together and focus on the end results.

Remember that to being a 'Dynamic Duo' takes courage and effort.

All your 'clarity', 'commitment', 'communication' and 'cooperation' as a team will be the foundations for the vision you share together. Collaborating on your combined dreams only serves to strengthen the foundations of everything you have built together.

I strongly believe that if two people put their hearts and minds together, they can achieve the most amazing things.

Growing together

To ensure your journey together is long and fruitful, you both need to be able to learn and grow as individuals as well as a couple. You don't want one person heading off without the other on a new pathway or journey.

By now you probably understand who you are, and where you are going on this journey together. However, being individual people within each partnership, you will learn and grow at different times and at different rates, much of which is factored in by your own emotional intelligence and your openness to learning.

Like anything, if one person is learning and the other is not, eventually you will drift apart. One will progress, while the other will remain at the sidelines, watching everyone else around them shift and change.

The only way that I have found to ensure that we are both learning and growing is to be connected to myself and help my husband become more connected to himself too. From there, everything else flows. While I have no ultimate control over my husband's journey, I can at least be aware of the things that I can do to support and encourage his learning.

For myself, I have greater insight into things that directly affect my life, and insight into the parts of my relationship with my husband that may impact our romance or our business together. I am conscious of disruptions to our relationship and make it a priority to address any issues that may take us off track or deteriorate our relationship, romance or ability to communicate.

The journey is not an easy one to take, because you will need courage to ask yourself the tough questions such as, 'What do you really want?' It also takes strength to accept the answer, even when it may be different to what you have been trying to hold together all these years.

Take time out and be gentle on yourself, and work together through things that may need addressing in your relationship or the business. Remember that this process can take months or even years to make the necessary adjustments, which is great, because it allows for both of you to work through your separate issues as well as the combined challenges together. Supporting each other is much easier with unconditional love and a non-judgmental attitude.

If you have ever looked into the eyes of a baby, you will notice that they are wide, exploring, soaking up the world around them with all the sights and sounds, colours and movement. They look at the world in awe and wonder. They are captured by learning, as they find themselves taking in every experience. The baby is actually open to learning by nature.

As humans, we are probably at our most connected to ourselves when we are babies; however, we tend to lose that connection as we grow. By the time we reach our early teenage years, we are more impacted by our desire to connect with other people rather than ourselves. When we become adults and the stresses of life have all but consumed us, we have lost touch with who we are, which is why this process is so important for both partners in any partnership.

Be patient with the process, but don't shy away from the important things that come up. Address each and every aspect of your relationship, and make this a priority in both of your lives. Once you are committed to the relationship and the lines of effective communication are open, then cooperation and collaboration should come much easier.

Each day you have the chance to learn and grow within yourself. You can choose to make the most of these opportunities, or you can let them pass us by. For every situation, there are opportunities to change, and this will affect the rest of your lives together. While something so small and insignificant may not feel important at the time, the slightest gesture could mean the difference in ability and attitude much further down the road.

Exit strategy

At some point in time, you are going to want to get off the merry-go-round that is your business. Either you become too old to work, or you find that you are just 'over it'. So you will need to discuss an 'exit strategy' with your partner. One of the most important things is to address this as part of the initial business-planning phase.

It is never a priority when you are starting out in business, but regardless of what type of business it is, there needs to be a discussion about the 'end game'. What is your exit strategy going to be?

If your business is your livelihood, and you are hoping to leave it for the kids, make sure that you ask them if they even want to take over the family business. Whatever the situation, you have to plan for the day you will no longer be in your business.

You may wish to sell the business, in which case your business plan and visions will be different, as ultimately you will want to ensure that you build strong foundations for your legacy to pass to new owners when you retire.

Every person's 'exit strategy' will have a different set of objectives during the functioning and operation of the business. It is important to plan ahead for the desired outcome together, so that you can build the business appropriately for the day when you both decide to leave.

SUMMARY

So how do the successful people get to where they are?

As questioned earlier: do they connect with themselves first, and find out who they truly are and what their place in the world is? Or does the success come first, and then they find themselves? We cannot wait for the success, so we may as well start getting to know and connect with ourselves first.

I believe that there is no better way to live our lives than by sharing a business journey with someone we love dearly and can work well together to build a future that benefits both. Your family shares in your success, and you can enjoy the fruits of our labour together.

As with anything in life, there is no magic pill that will fix all your problems. Part of the process is about learning who you and your partner are as individuals, and then deciding who you want to become as a couple, and then taking it one step further by working together to build a business. By taking part in a business journey together, you will experience the satisfaction of creating something that you can be proud of *together*.

Remember, the money earned from your business is not the be all and end all. If your romance suffers as a result, then you lose it all and have to start again. Take care of your relationship first, and then work together on the business as a second priority. Never lose sight of the fact that you are in it together.

Having **clarity** around yourself and your partner's strengths and weaknesses brings a certain humility to living that recognises and accepts that you are both human beings doing the best you can with what you know at the time.

Where you strive to be different is through your love and **commitment** to each other in the relationship and in business, building something together that will create a strong and solid future.

The fulcrum to anything in the journey between love and business is through effective **communication**. Together you can resolve and solve any challenge that comes your way as you face this world of business and partnerships together. Let it be you and your partner against the world, not you against your partner.

Being part of a committed partnership requires not only some sacrifice, but also the ability to work well together as a team. Anticipating each other's move and **cooperating** together ensures that you can support and build on the efforts and momentum that will carry your business journey further and faster to success.

Creating your common visions is the ultimate satisfaction when you can both **collaborate** your efforts, maximising your results, and you can turn to each other at the end of the day and say, 'Isn't this an awesome life we have together?'

Whatever your journey is, I wish you and your family every success for the future of your relationship and your business efforts together.

Julie Richman

ADDITIONAL INFORMATION

Recommended reading

- Alan and Barbara Pease – *Why Men Don't Listen and Women Can't Read Maps*
- Gary Chapman – *The 5 Love Languages*
- Michael E. Gerber – *The E Myth* (Original and the revisited version)
- Gary Zukav – *The Heart of the Soul*
- Andrew Fuller – *Tricky People*
- Andrew Griffiths – *101 Ways to Have a Business and a Life*
- Daniel Priestly – *Key Person of Influence*
- Dan Millman – *The Laws of Spirit*

Recommended viewing

- Mark Gungor – 'Laugh Your Way to a Better Marriage' (YouTube series)
- Dynamic Duos – 'Interviews with Real Business Couples' (Podcast series)

Check your 'Ultimate Potential' with our FREE Compatibility Report

How well do you and your partner work together in a business?

Where do you feel that your business life or relationship could be better?

Improve your love life AND grow your business happily together!

Find new ways to reach the untapped potential by applying teamwork strategies, learning about your relationship and growing a strong business platform together.

Your personalised results uncover each partnership's compatibility and capacity to work together in business through a series of key questions.

This comprehensive analysis takes an insightful diagnostic approach from both aspects of a relationship. The compatibility report brings to the forefront, any potential areas that may present challenges if not addressed. The results uncover the strengths and weaknesses in each couples attitude and ability to collaborate on the ultimate vision of becoming a successful Dynamic Duo Couple.

> **FOR YOUR FREE REPORT**
>
> Click on the following website link:
> www.dynamicduotest.com.au

Find ways to enhance happiness, motivation, success and closeness in your love life, and your business efforts.

Couples who combine their efforts, can magnify their end results exponentially.

Live your dreams together!

Julie Richman

Dynamic Duos in Business presents

REIGNITE
Weekend Workshop

Come along and share the fun and exciting discoveries during our couples in business Reignite weekend.

Register your interest here: www.dynamicduos.com.au/reignite
Secure your place and receive a 20% discount.
Code: ReigniteUs1 (code for discount is case sensitive).
2 days: 9 am – 4 pm (lunch included)
LIMITED SPACES AVAILABLE

We guarantee that you will learn new things about yourself and your partner. The Reignite Course will ensure that you will clarify your future, learn effective communication skills, work towards efficient teamwork, and build upon a strong foundation towards a brilliant business future together.

Things you will gain from the Reignite workshop:
- Rekindle the romantic spark in your relationship
- Discover greater communication skills and how to work effectively together
- Building a great future together through teamwork
- Gain business insights that helps to increase success and profitability in the immediate future

To register in your capital city visit www.dynamicduos.com.au/reignite

www.ingramcontent.com/pod-product-compliance
Lightning Source LLC
Chambersburg PA
CBHW051944290426
44110CB00015B/2102